I dedicate this to you, thank you so much for supporting my art <3

. ▪ ｡ . ▪ ° ♡▪+ ° ✧ ☾ ୭ .. : ° + ✿ ▪ ° ▪ ｡ .

Feel free to get any of these designs tattooed! Please tag me in a photo on instagram or a video on tik tok :)

ig- @bdaesthetic

tik tok- @thatgirlwhodoesart

You do NOT have my permission to sell these designs or profit off of them in any way! These are all copyrighted and you only have my permission to get a design done if you have bought this book.

stay positive and i hope your days are filled with peace and abundance.

. ▪ ｡ . ▪ ° ♡▪+ ° ✧ ☾ ୭ .. : ° + ✿ ▪ ° ▪ ｡ .

custom tattoo commission information:

My tattoo commission prices start at $15 and go up depending on difficulty. Price is determined based on size, detail, design style, and estimated time it will take me. Once you provide me with a description of your design idea, which includes:

- design idea
- what you would like to be included in the design
- size preference dimensions in inches
- your payment method (venmo, or paypal)

(you can also choose to give me complete artistic freedom!)

I will then provide you with the price of your commission. Once I receive your payment that includes your instagram handle in the description, I will begin working on your design. When your design is completed I will send the scanned image to you.(rotations are usually completely within 2-4 days) if I don't get back to you within 7 days I ask for you to message me again!

I ACCEPT CUSTOM TATTOO COMMISSION REQUESTS IN MY INSTAGRAM DMS @bdaesthetic

The rotations of dms are chosen randomly, the best way to get on my rotation is to message me every time I post that i'm accepting a new rotation on my instagram story.

PAYMENT METHODS-

venmo: Bailey-Drinkwater

paypal: BaileyDrinkwater

.·。.·° ♡·₊° ✧ ☾ ☽ . . : ° ₊ ✿ · ° ·。.

purchasing premade designs

If you like any of my designs i've posted on my tik tok or instagram, and would like to get them done as a tattoo; my premade designs are $5.

venmo or paypal me $5 and include a description of which design it is and your instagram handle!

I will then send you a scanned image of the design.

please make sure you spell your instagram handle correctly, otherwise there is no way i'd be able to find you

. ·ₒ . ·° ♡·₊°✧☾☽.. :°₊✿·° ·ₒ .

MONTHLY SURPRISE DESIGNS

Each month I will be doing a sale of premade suprise designs. I make a bunch of special designs and don’t post them on any of my social media. These designs are separated by themes for you to choose from.

I will post an announcement on my instagram when the sale is going on and all of the options of themes

for example

design 1-🦋☮🍄✨🌸

from there you can venmo or paypal me the price mentioned in the post, include your instagram handle in the description, and which design option you have chosen.

There will also be instructions when I make a post about the sale that you can follow, these are more general for you to understand the gist of the deal.

I make multiple designs of each them and will send whichever one I think resonates with you best based on your instagram profile

.▪｡.▪° ♡▪₊°✧ ☾୭..:°₊✿▪° ▪｡.

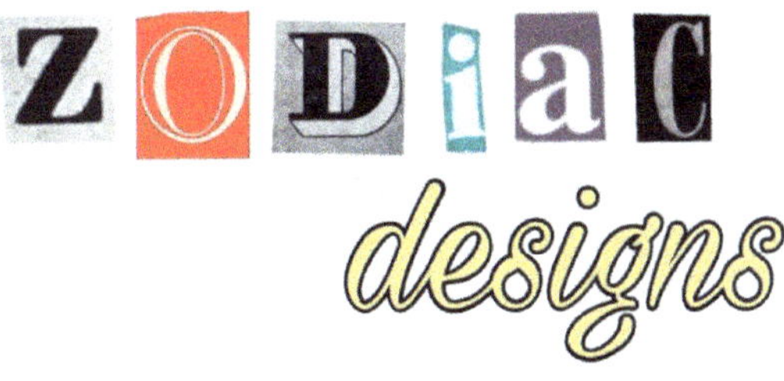
ZODiaC
designs

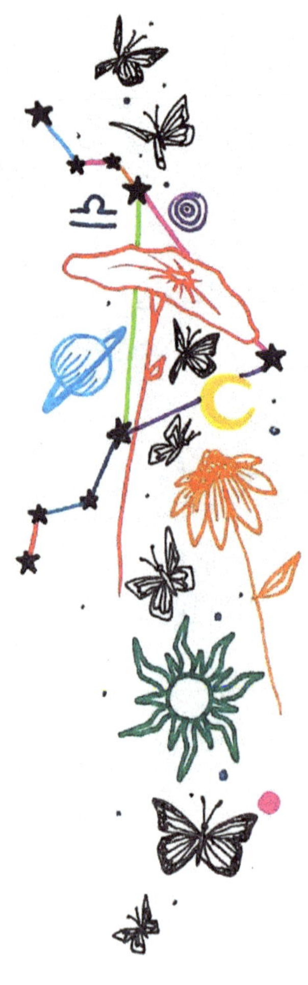

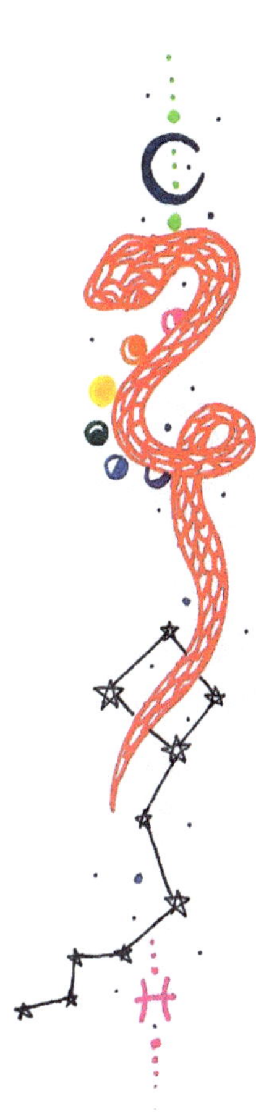

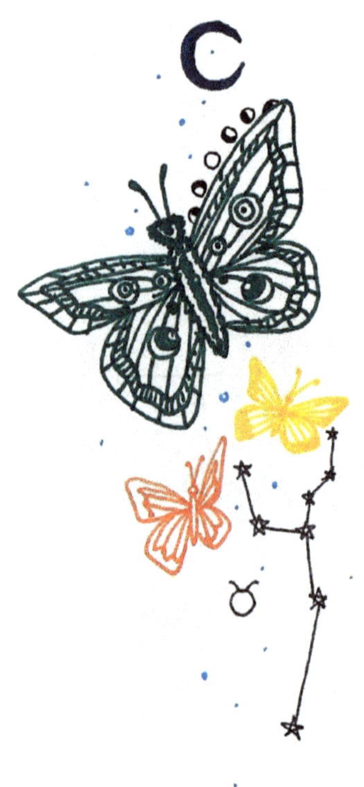

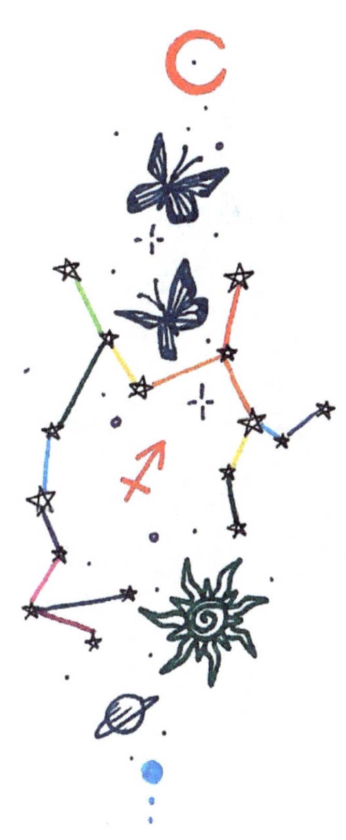

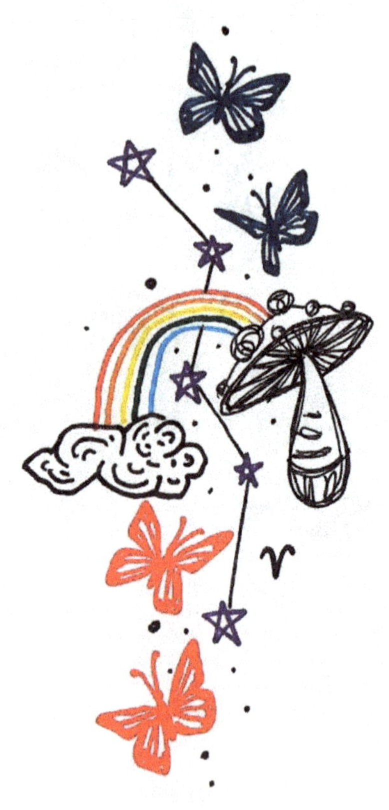

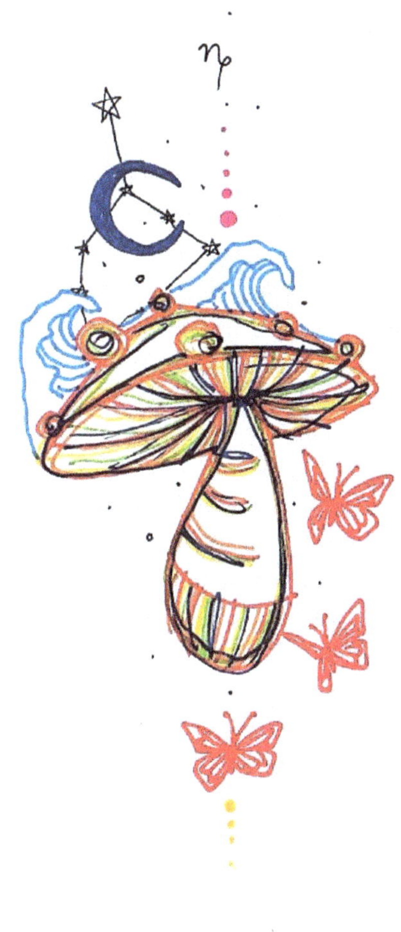

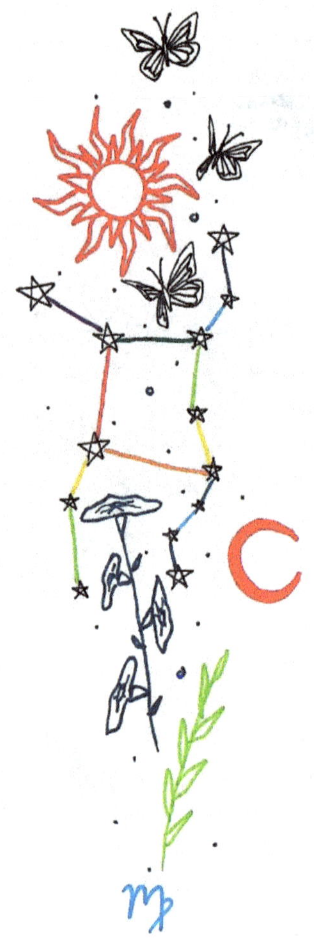

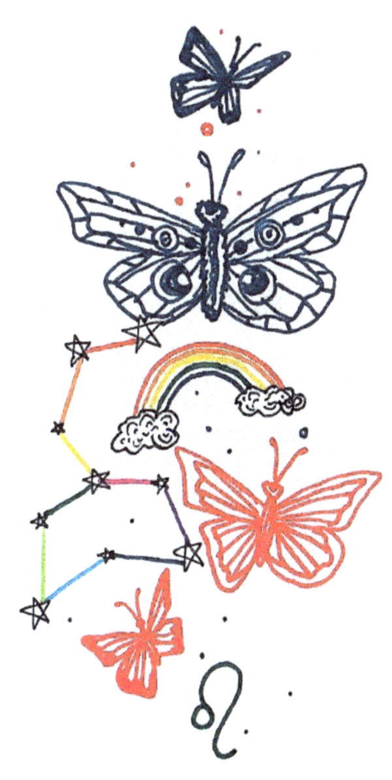

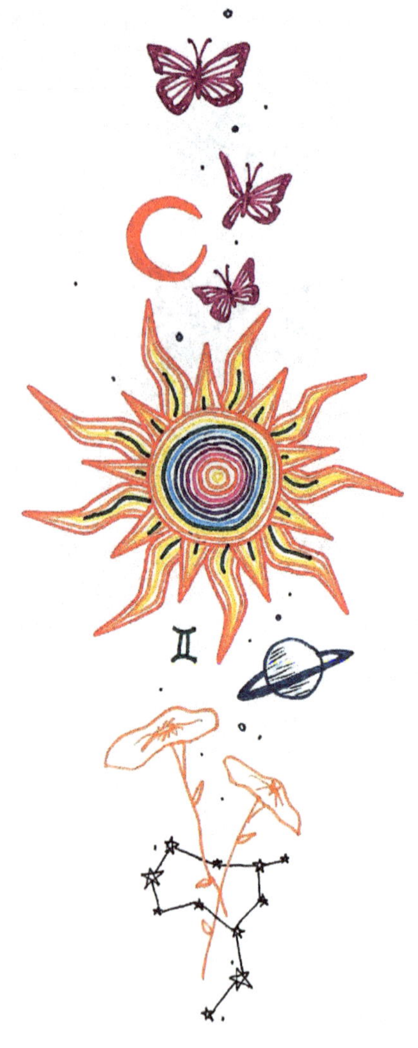

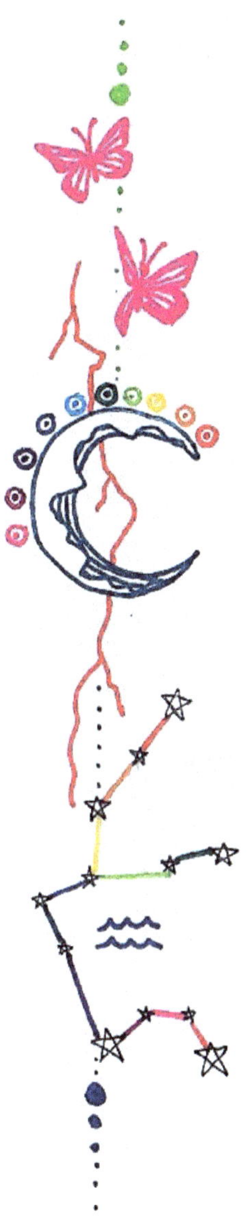

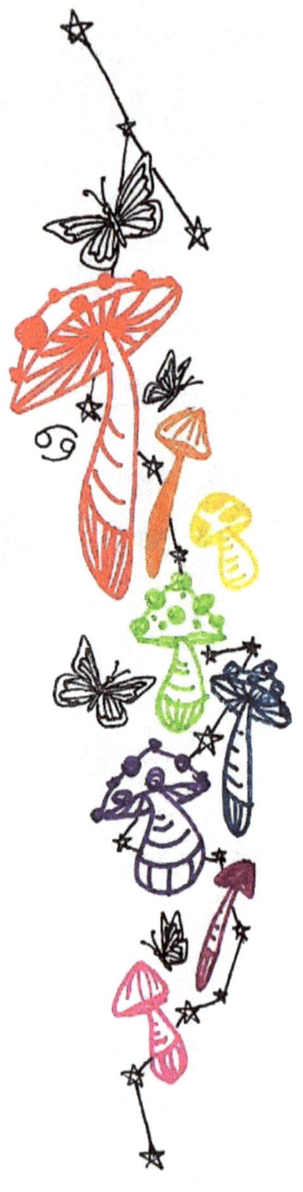

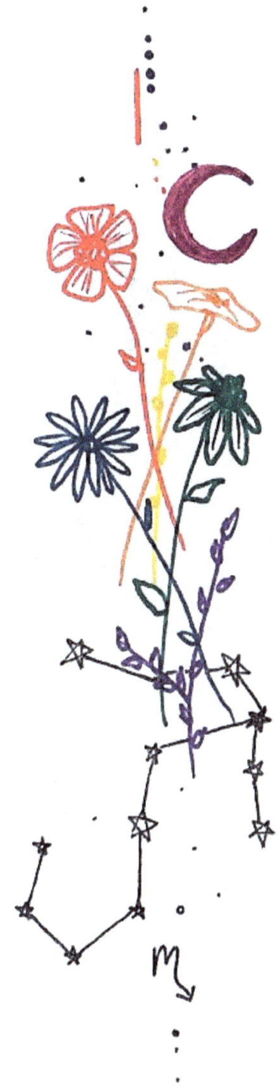

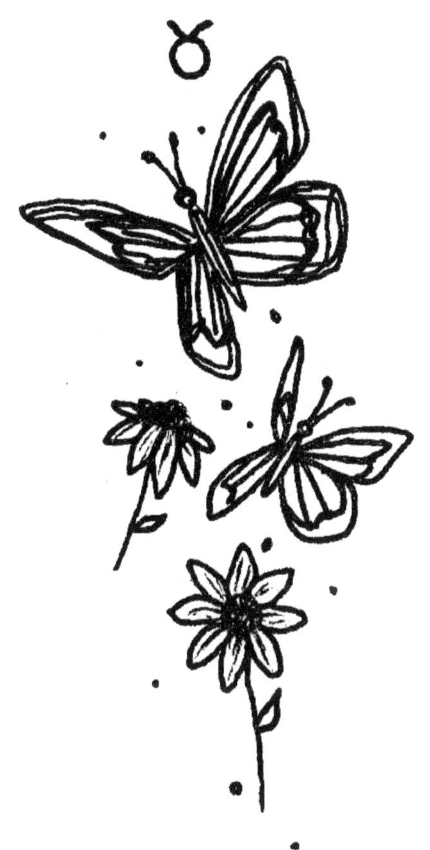

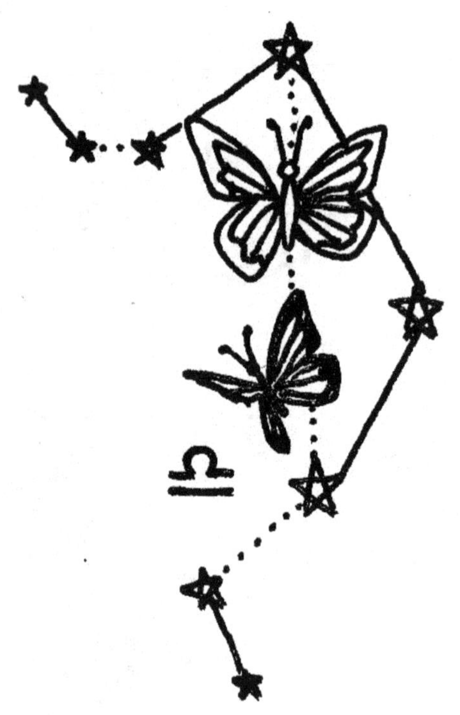

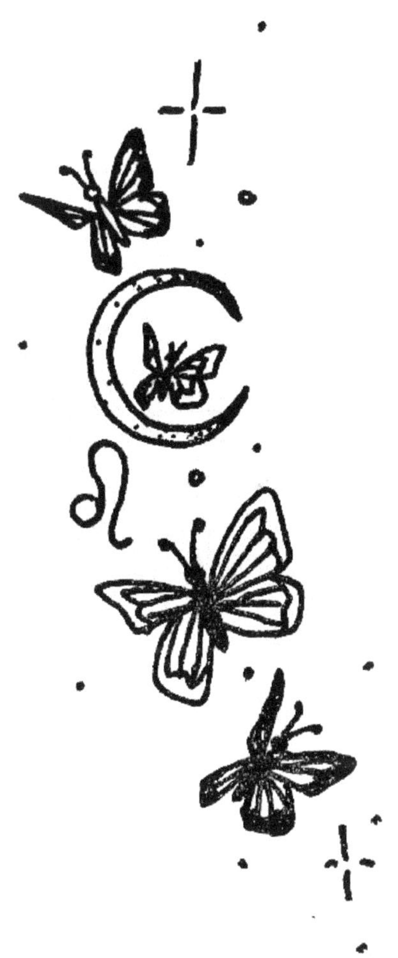

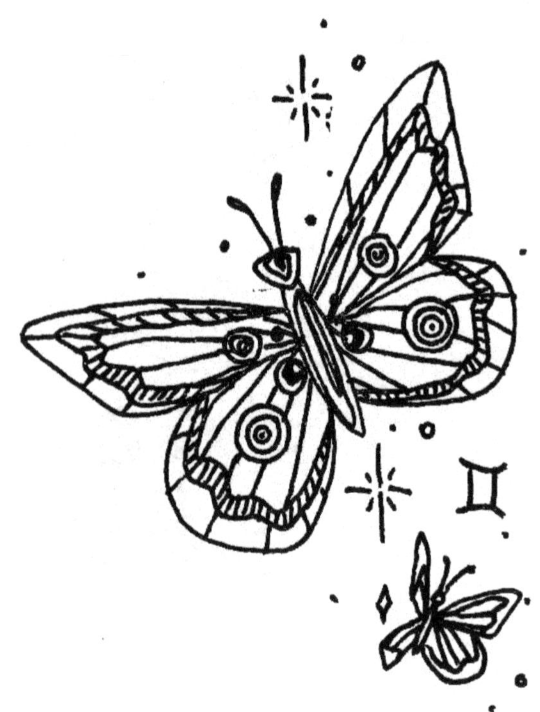

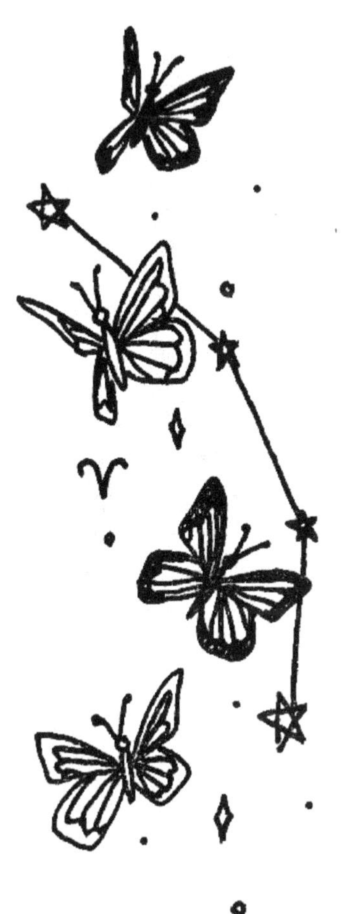

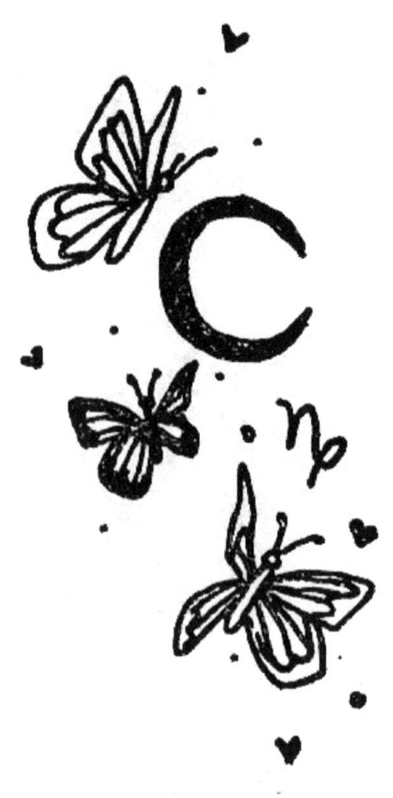

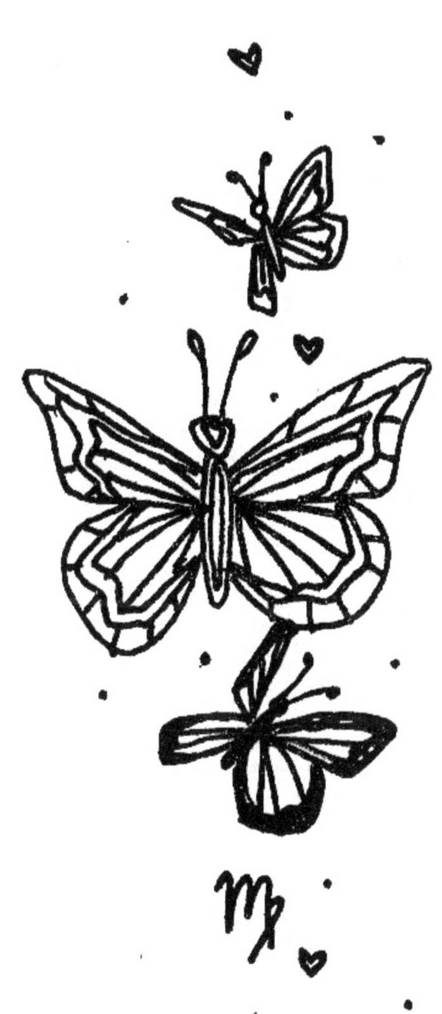

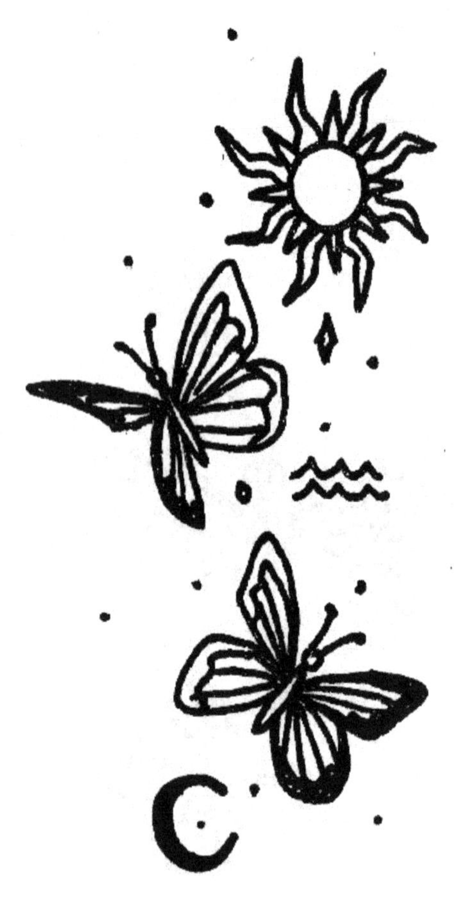

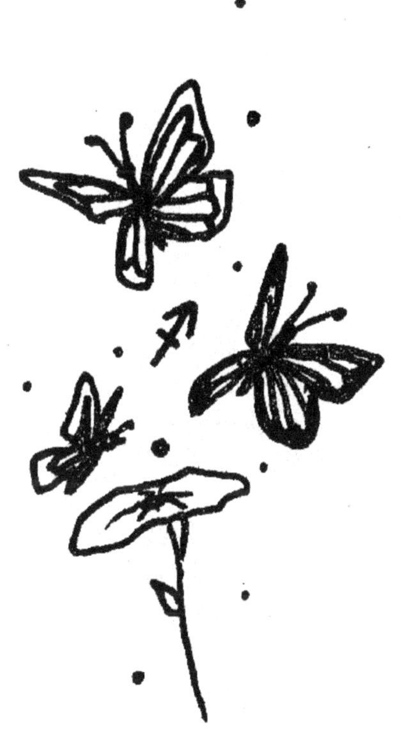

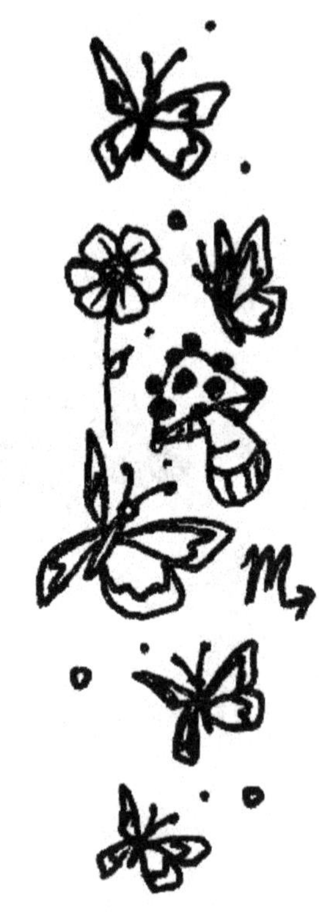

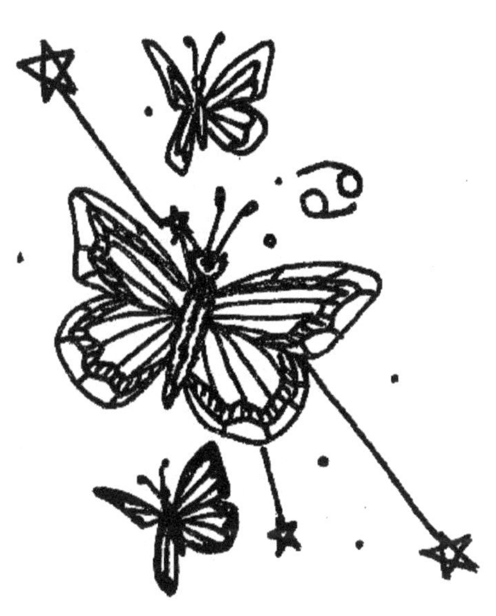

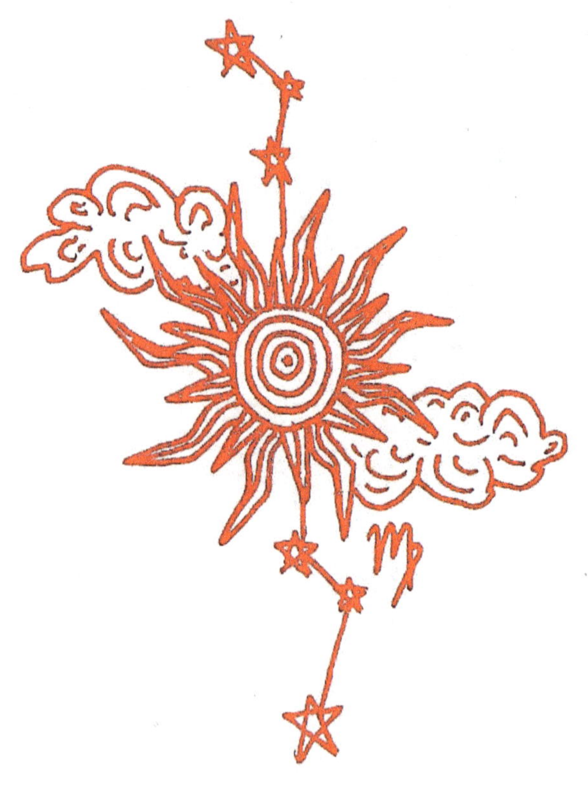

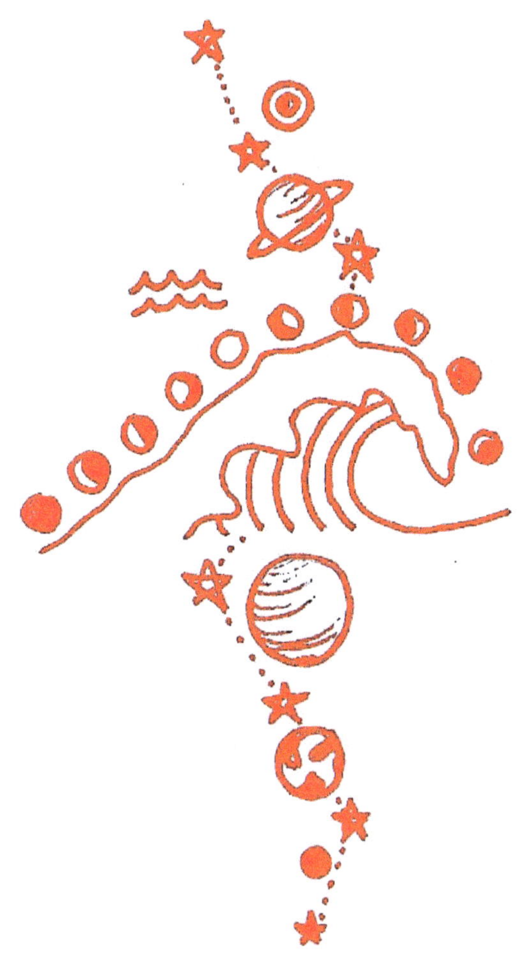

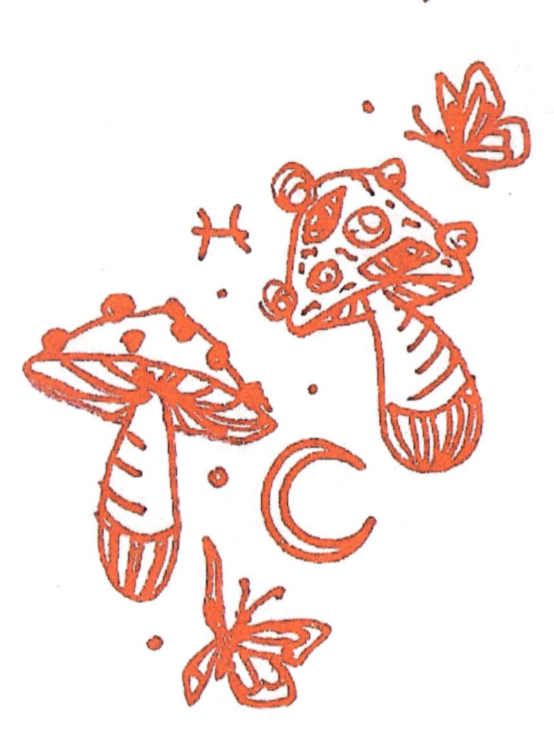

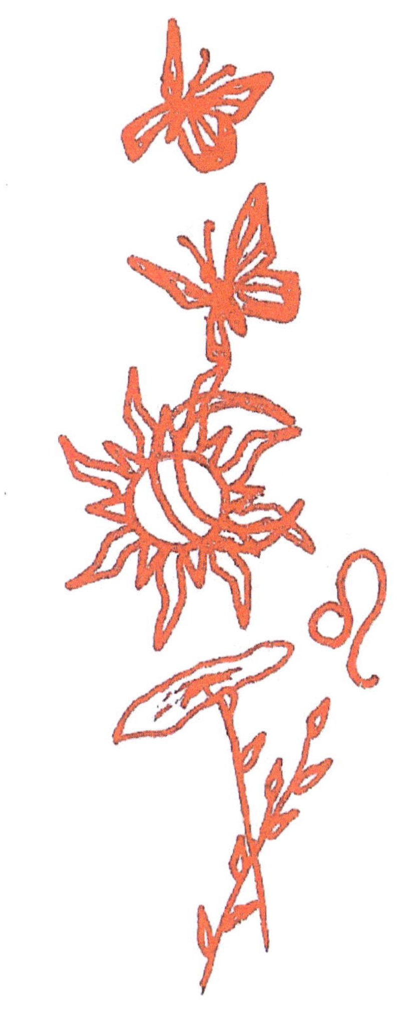

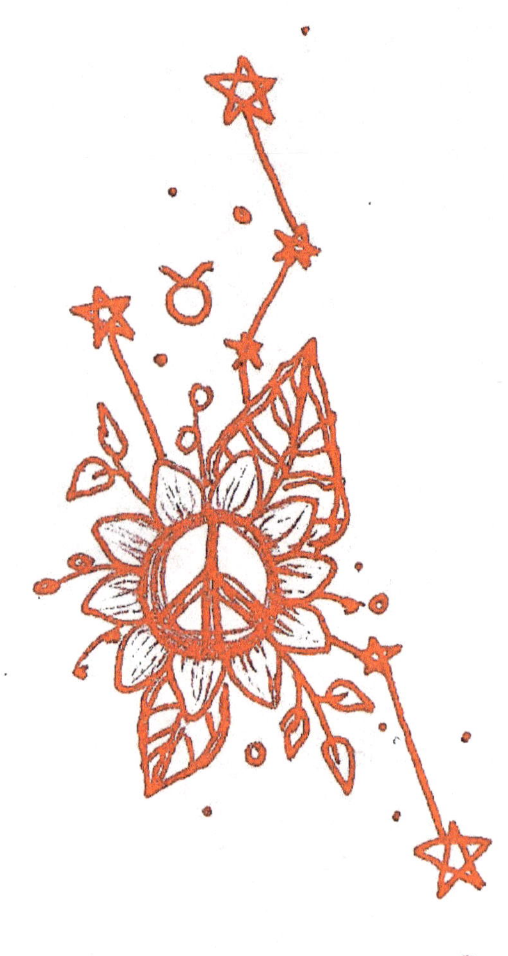

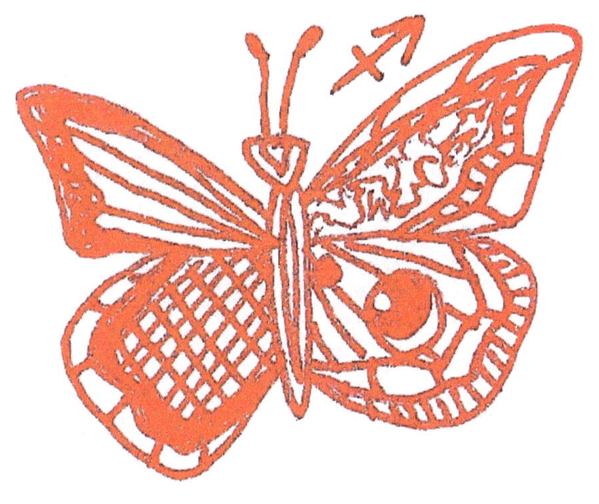

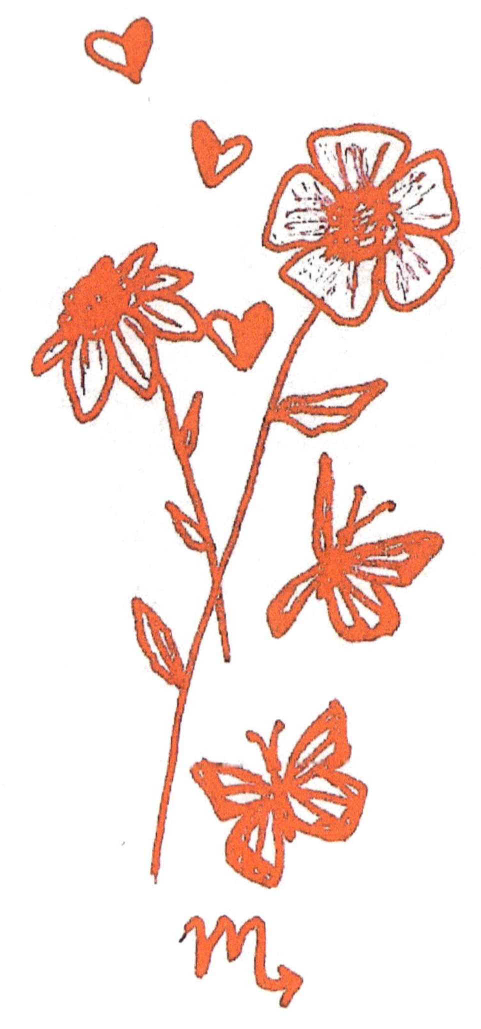

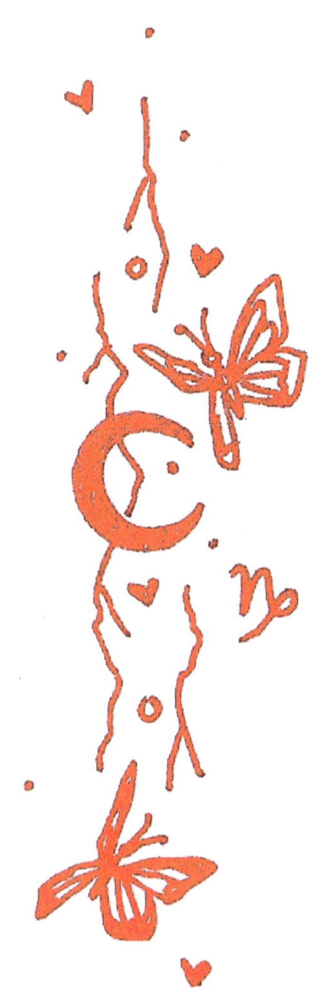

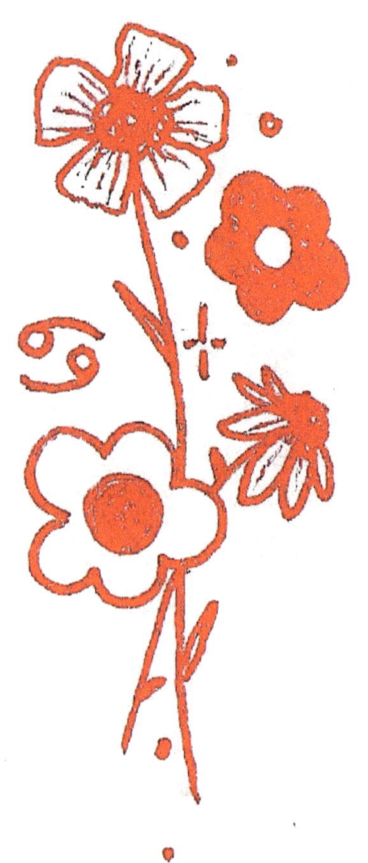

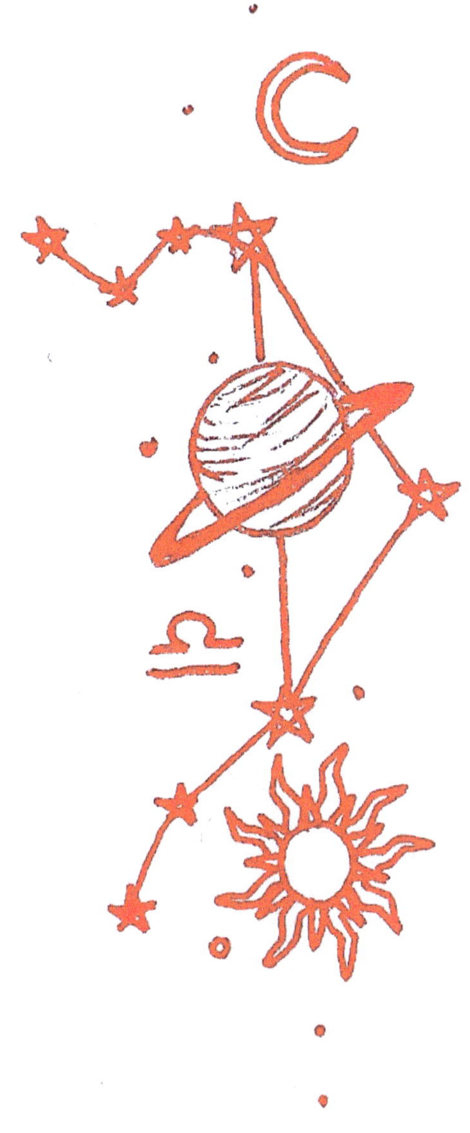

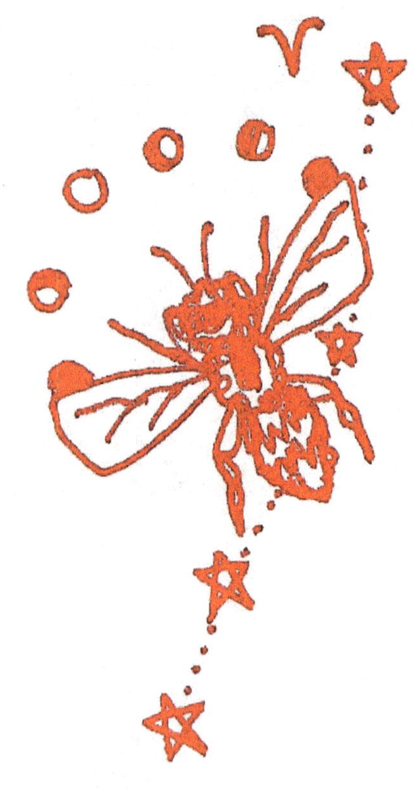

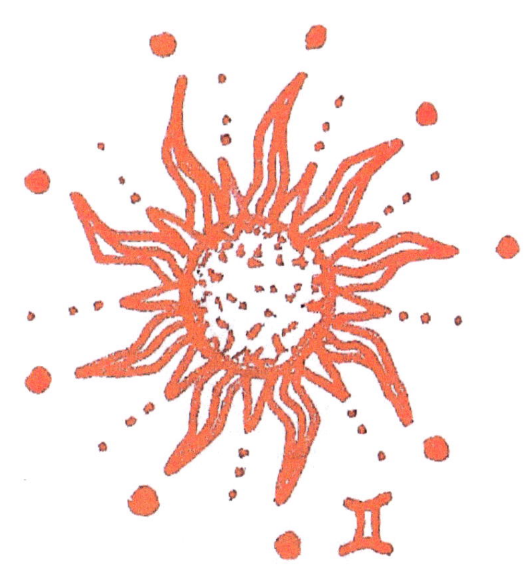

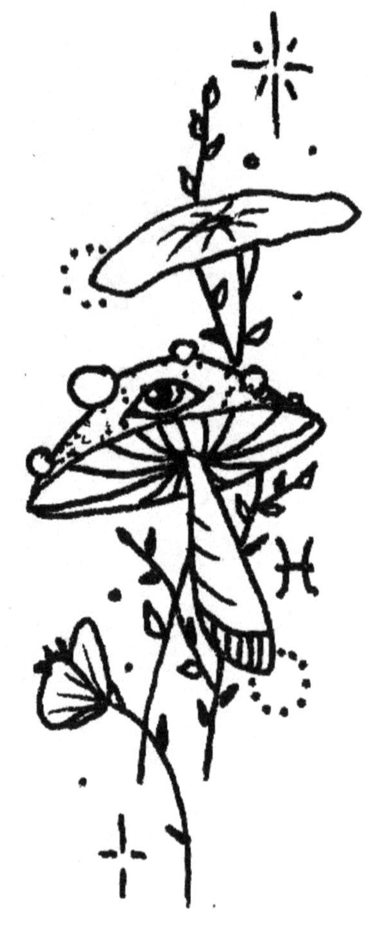

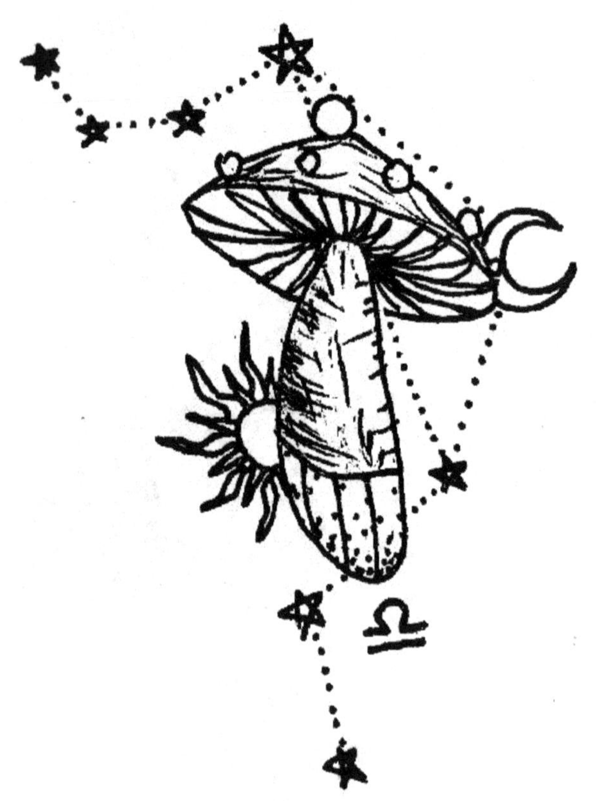

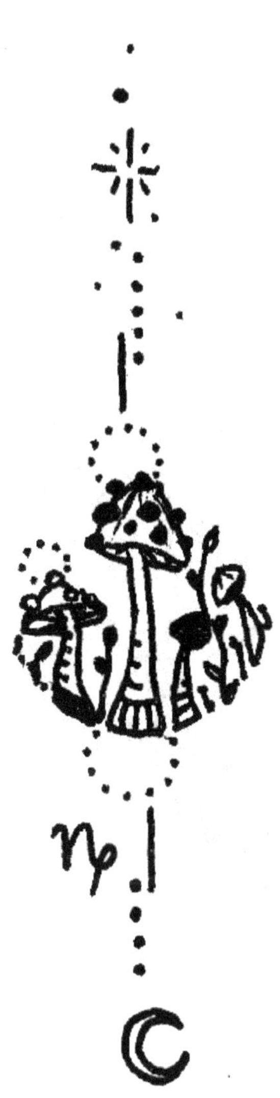

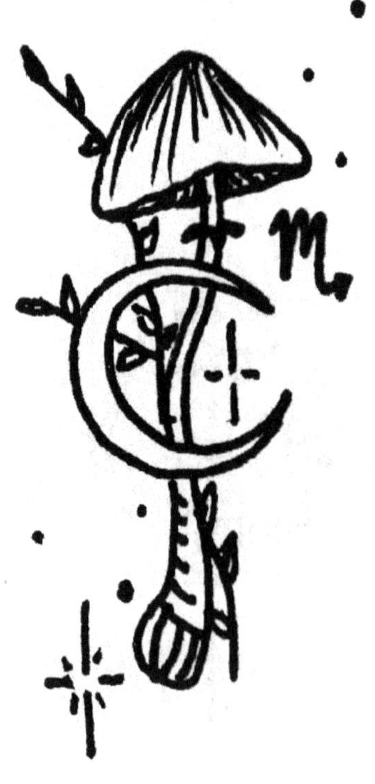

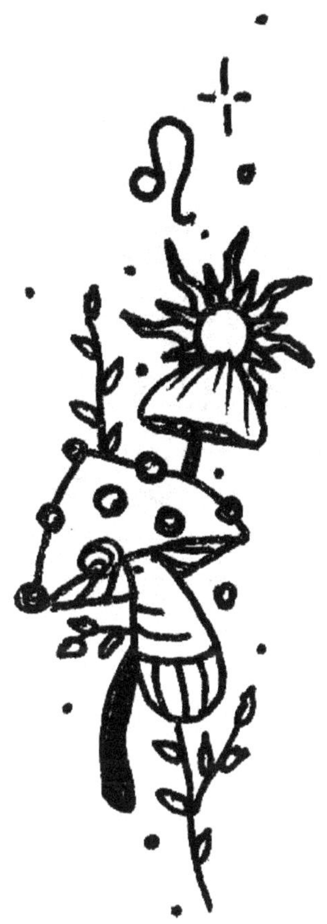

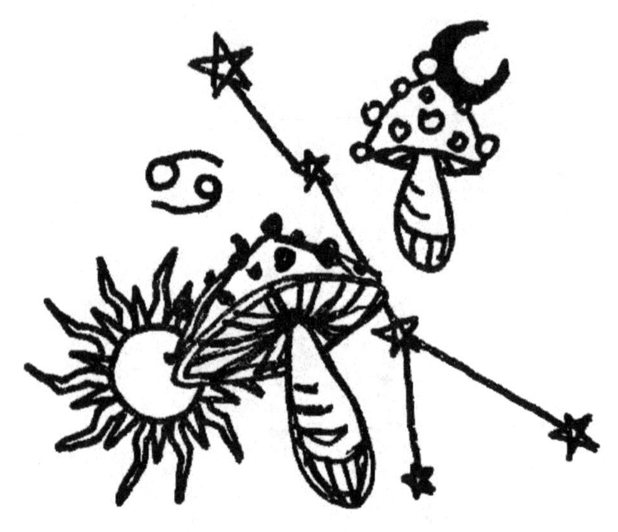

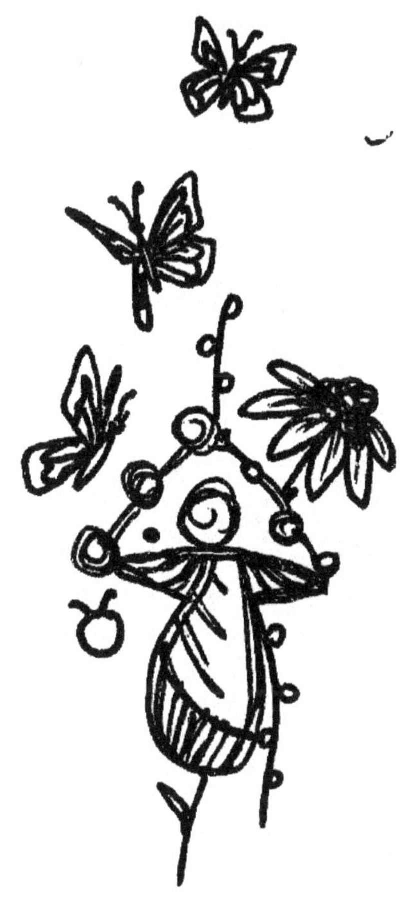

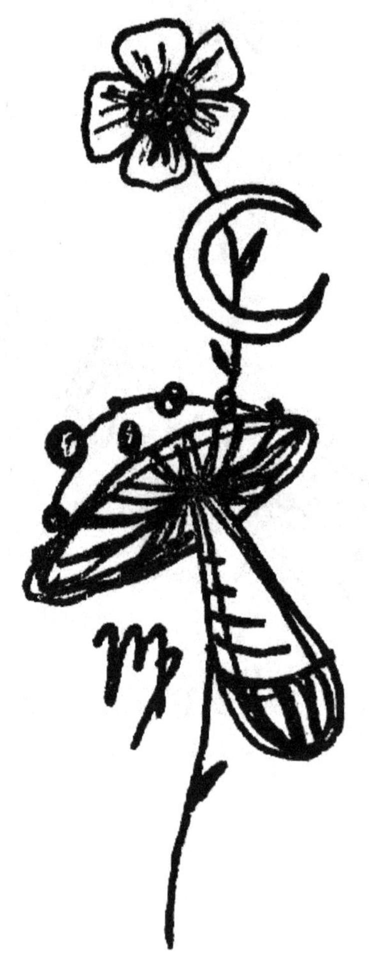

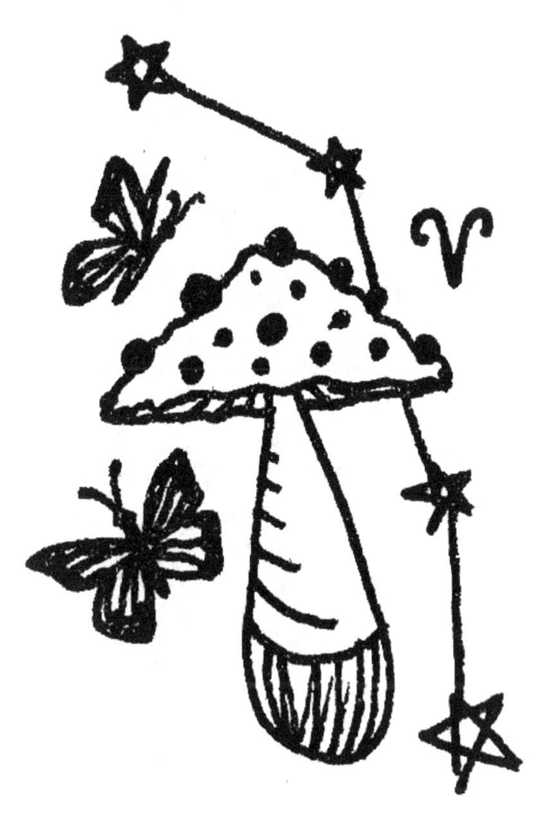

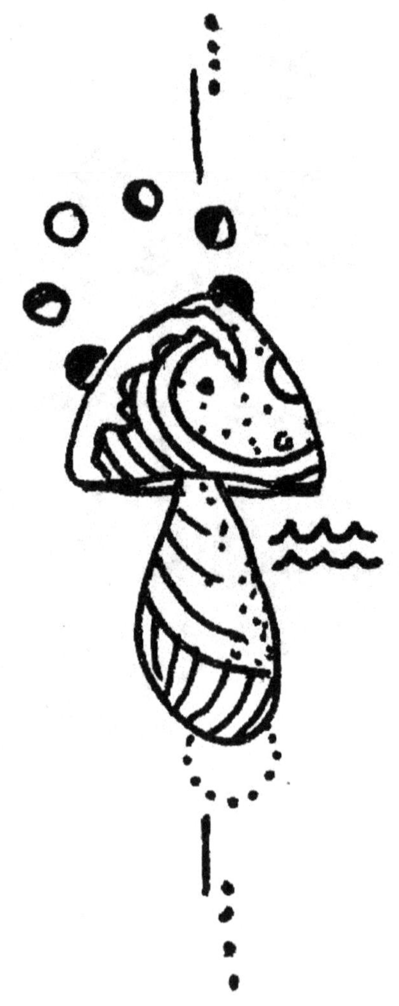

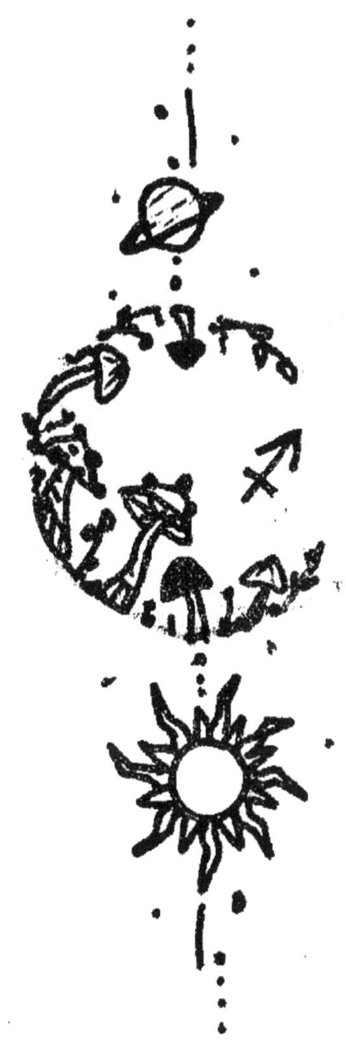

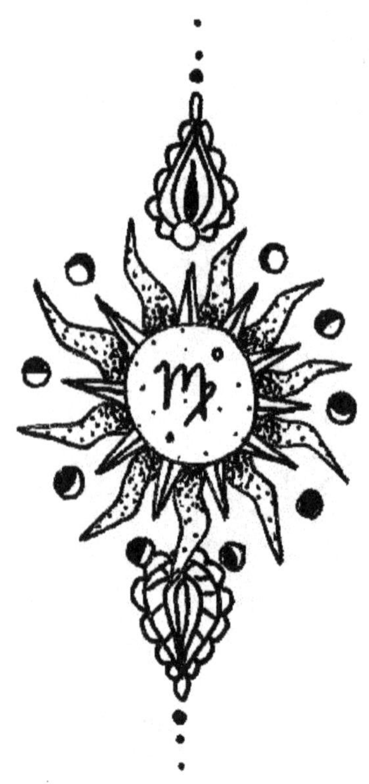

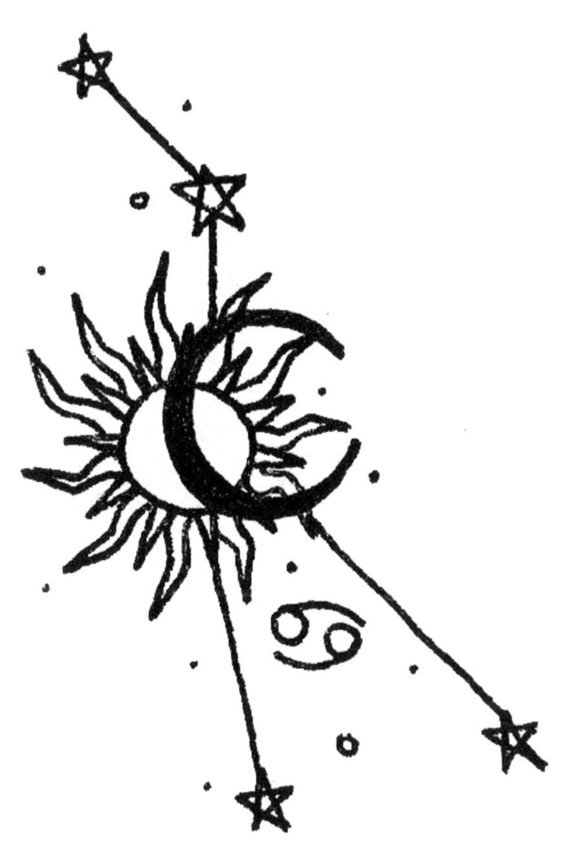

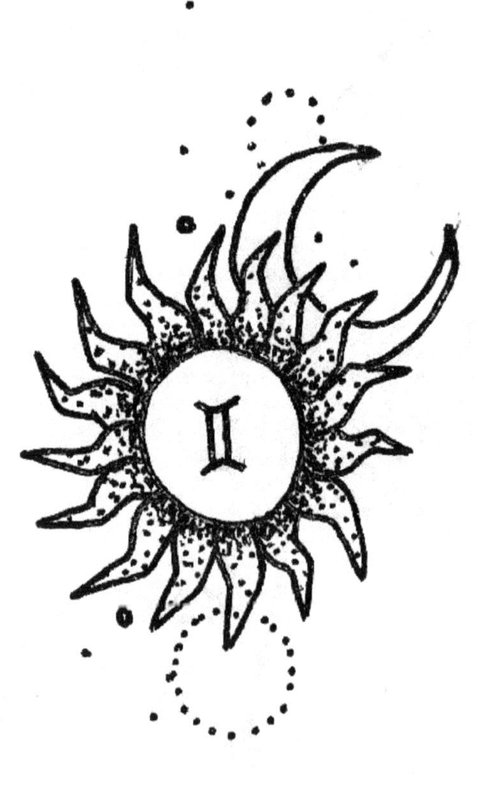

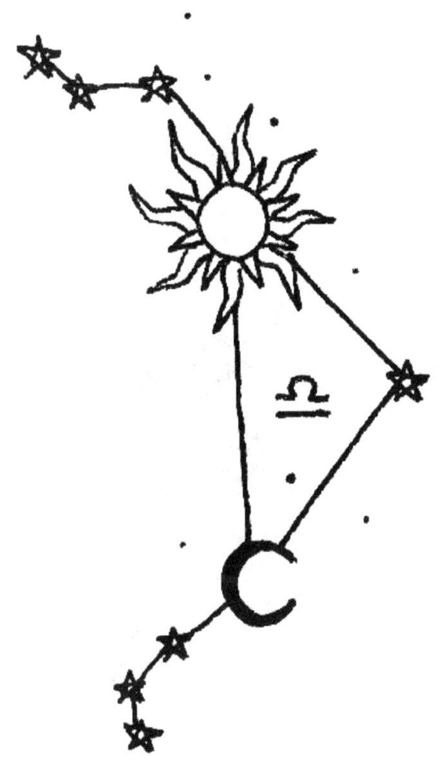

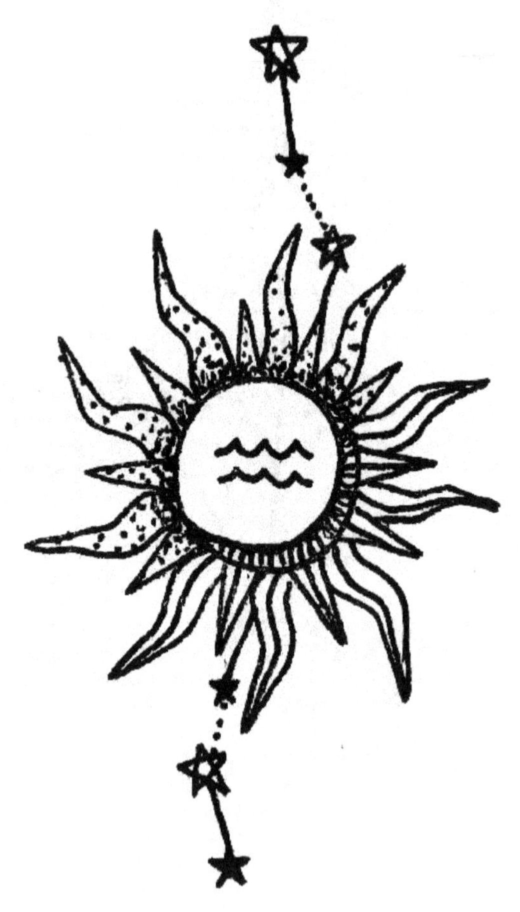

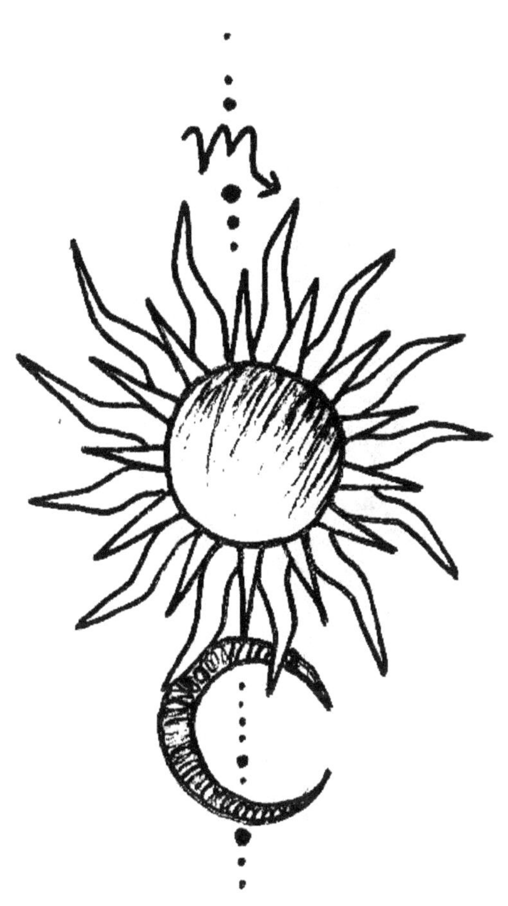

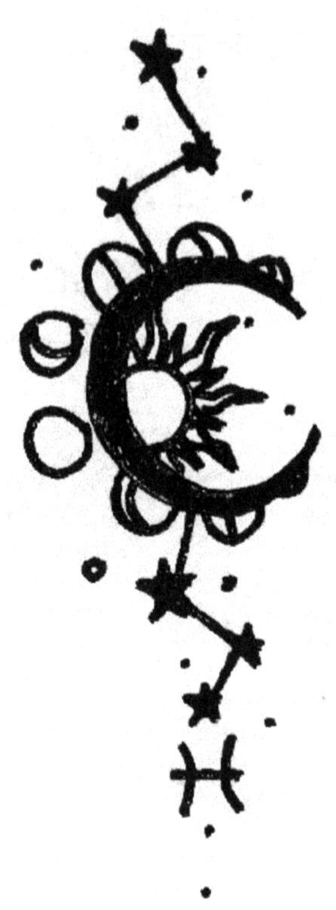

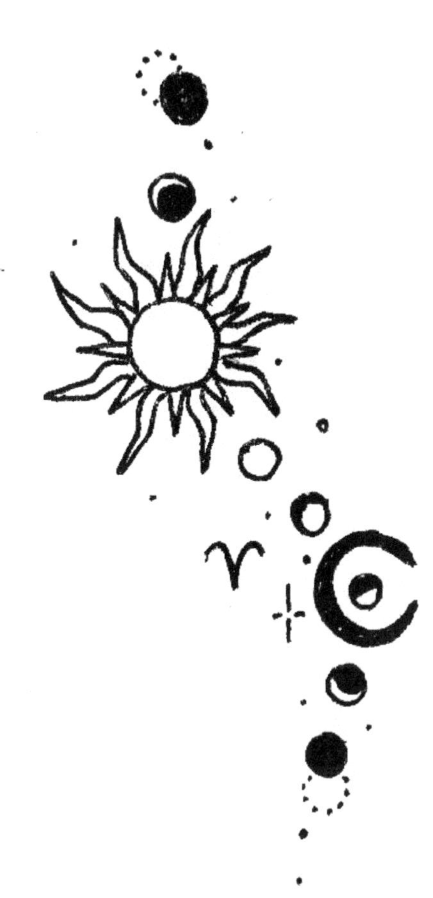

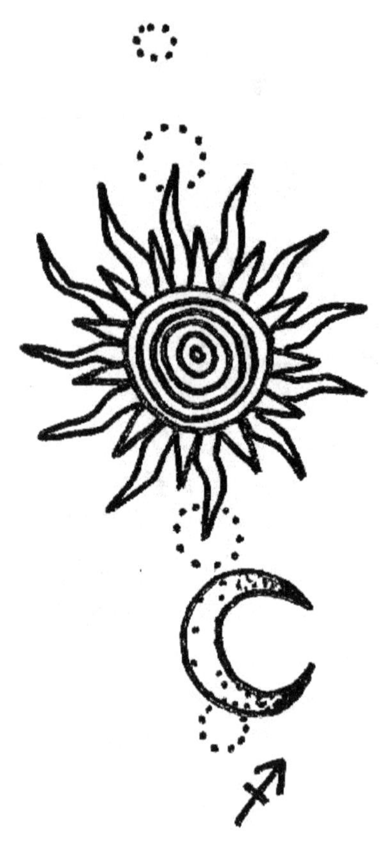

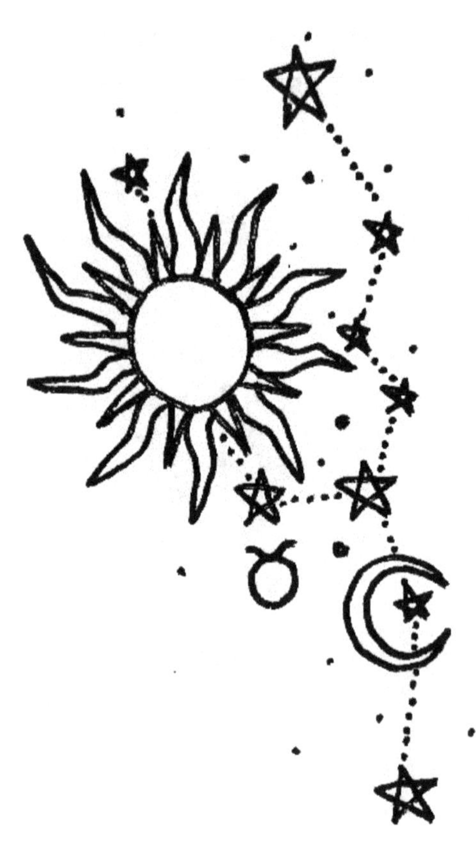

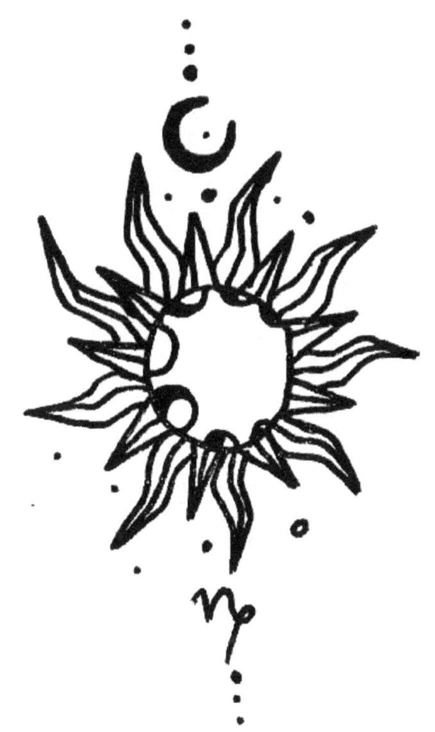

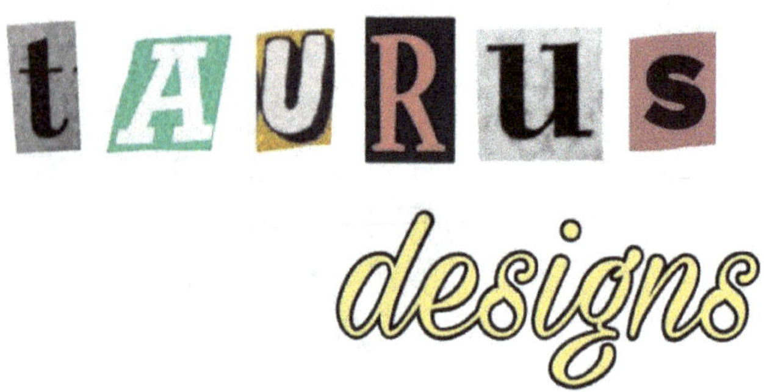
tAURUS
designs

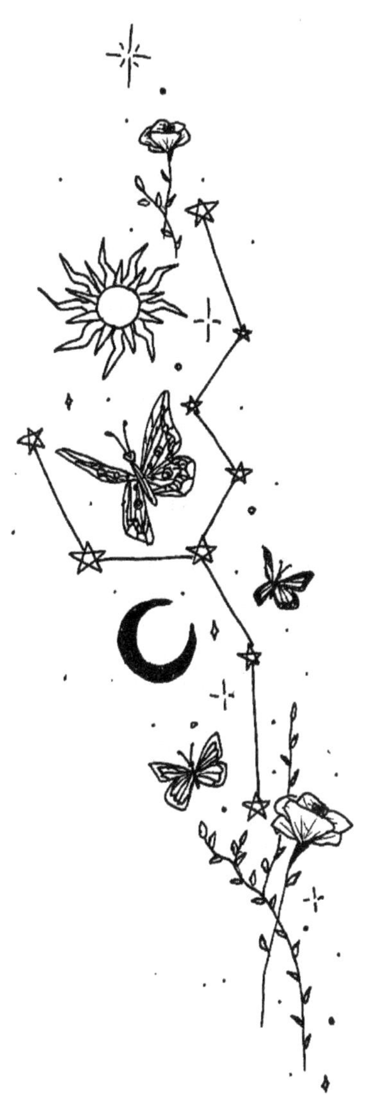

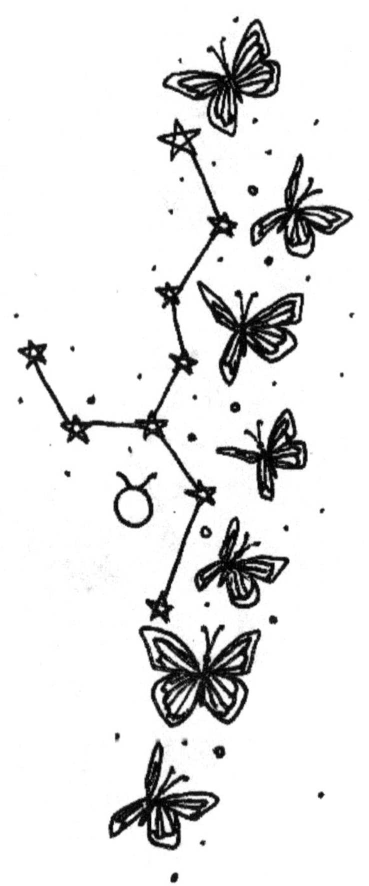

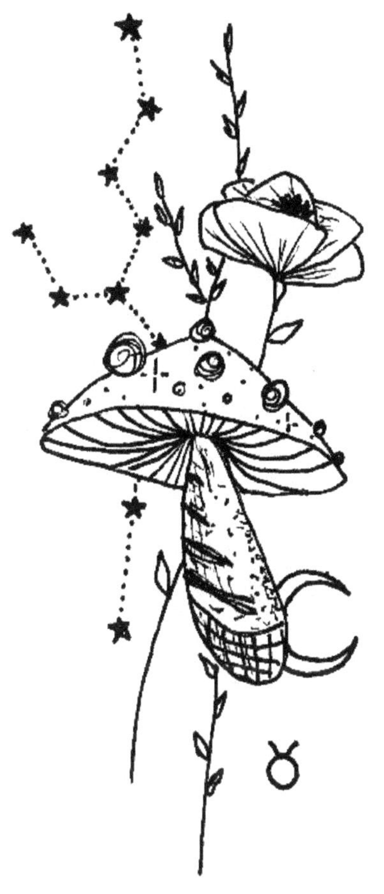

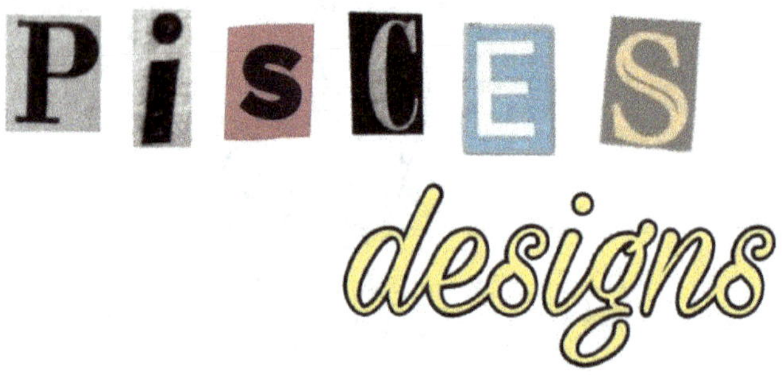
Pisces
designs

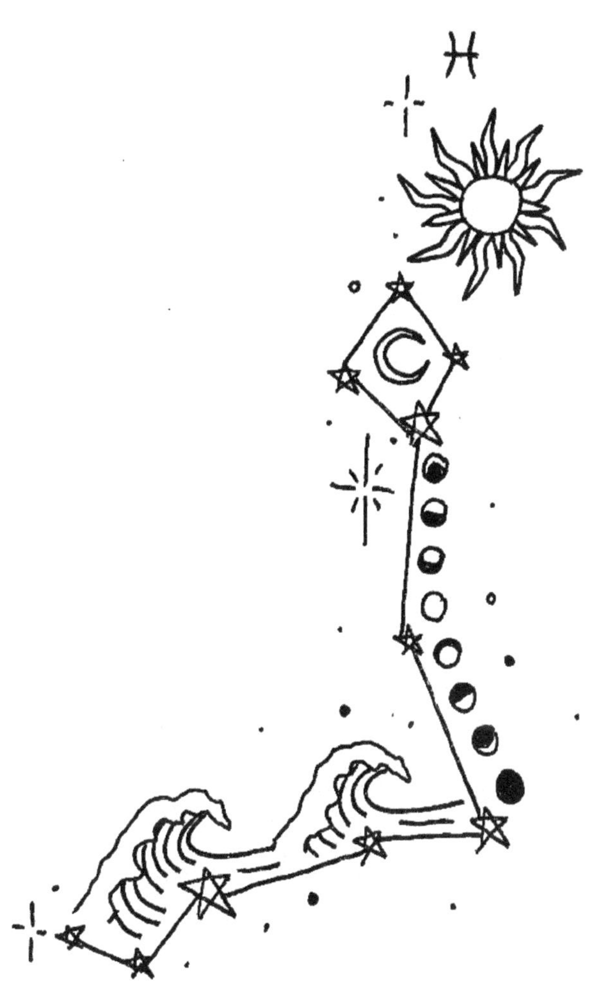

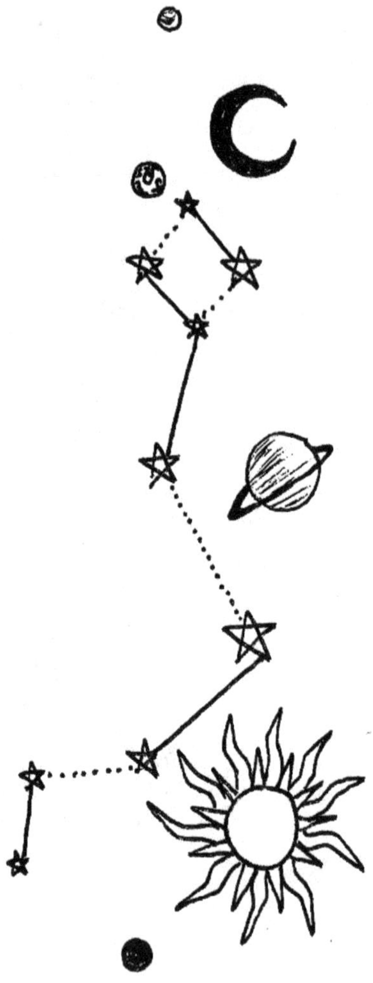

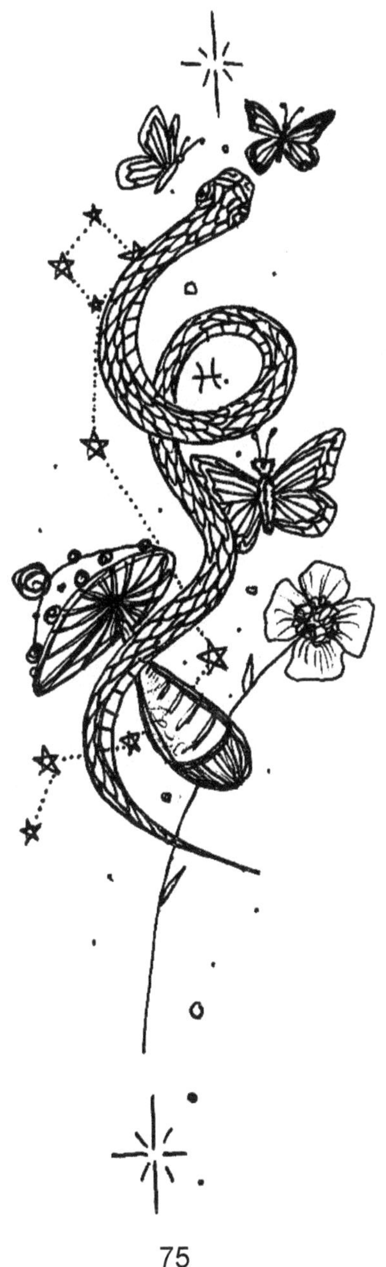

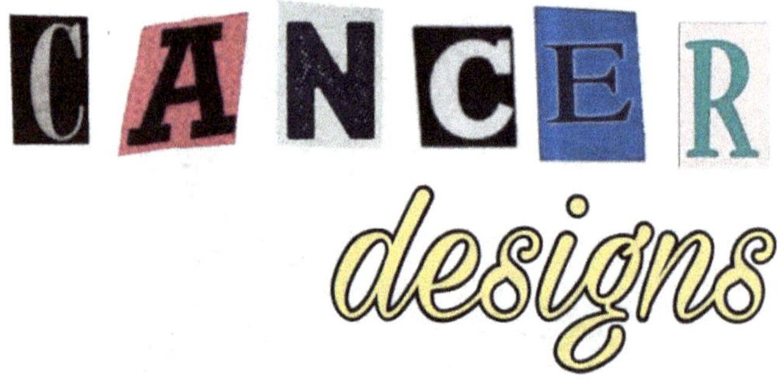
CANCER
designs

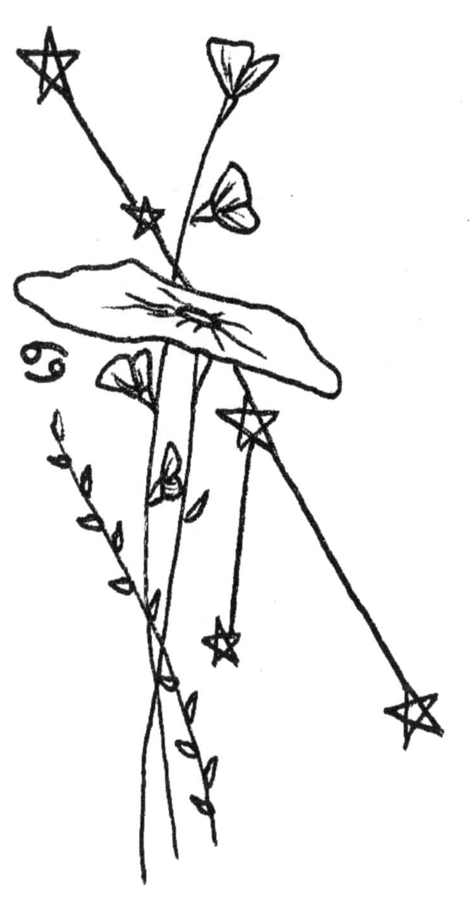

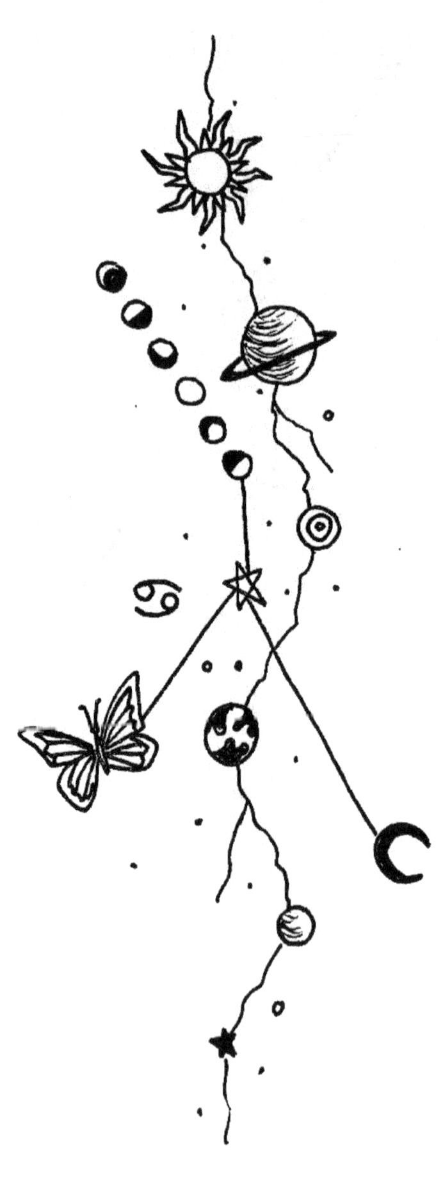

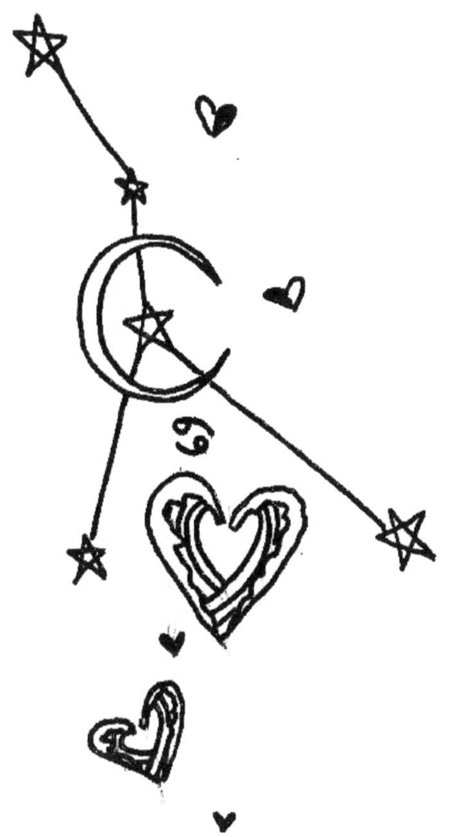

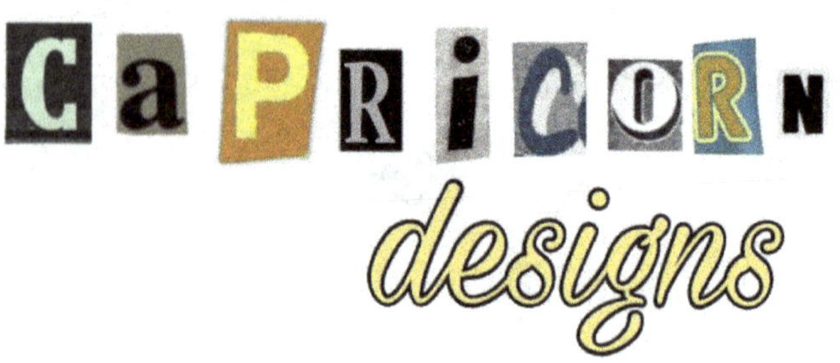
CaPRiCORN
designs

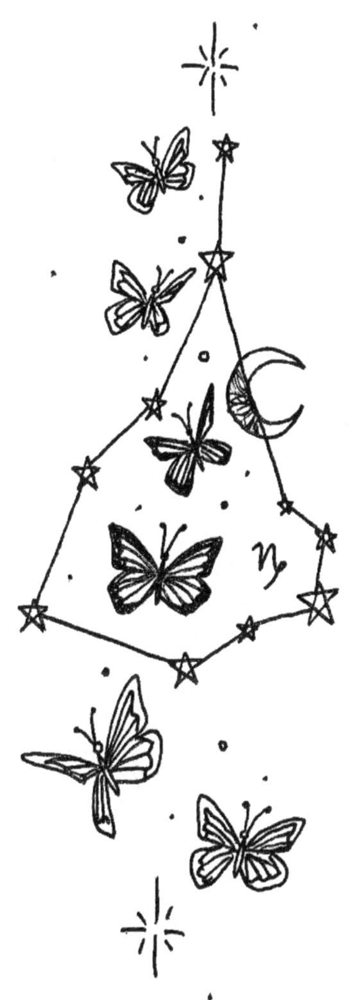

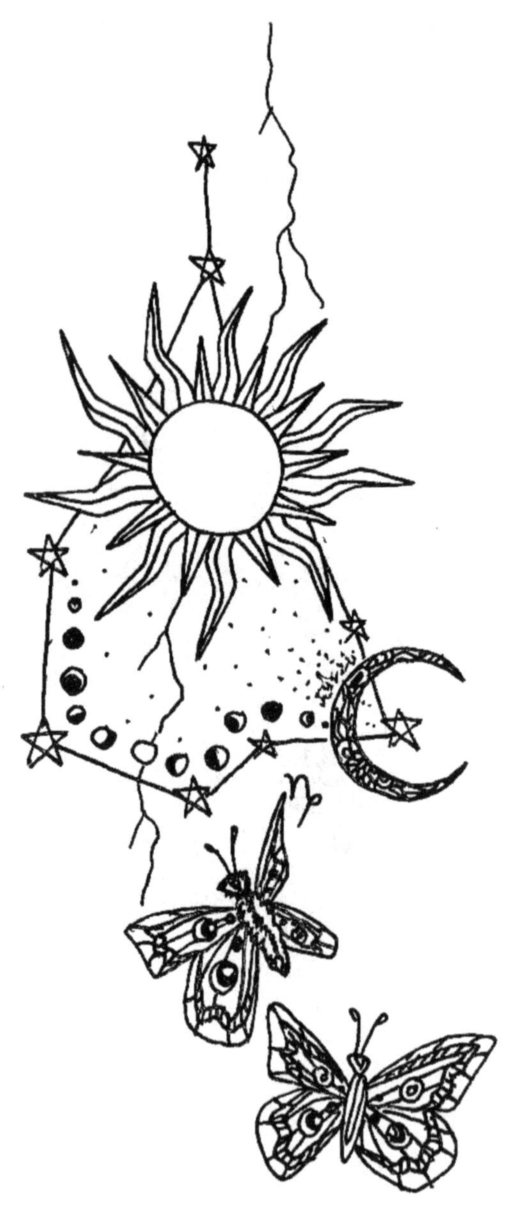

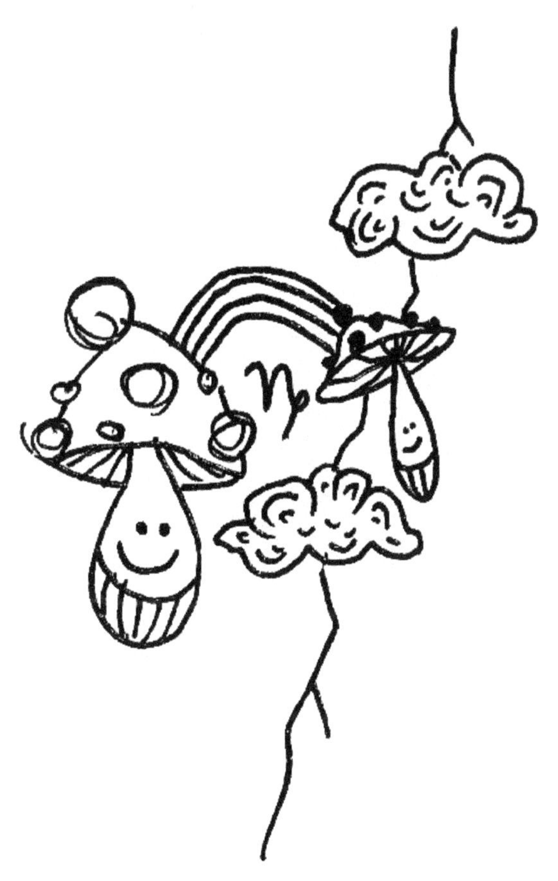

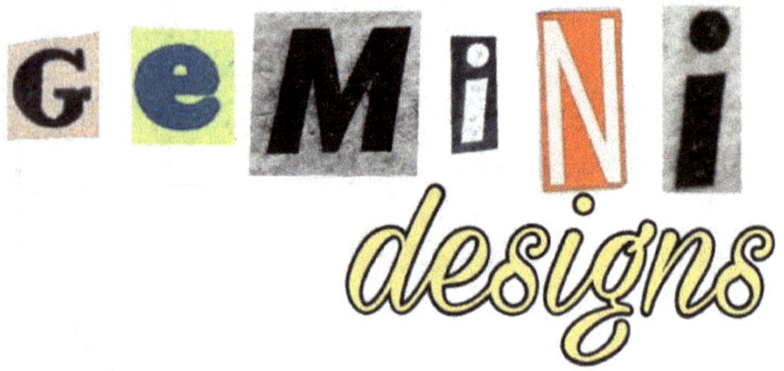
GeMiNi
designs

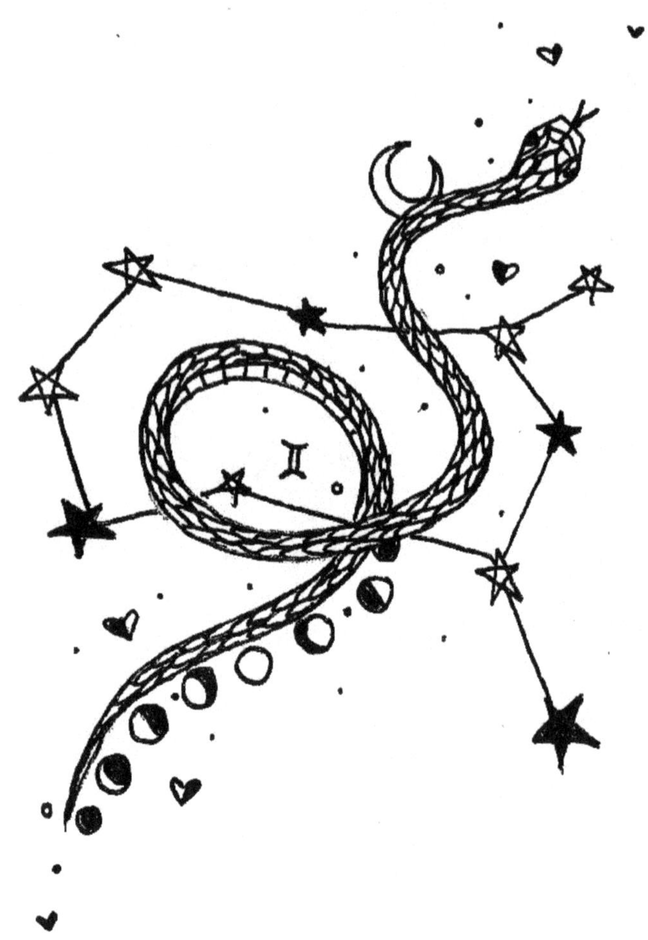

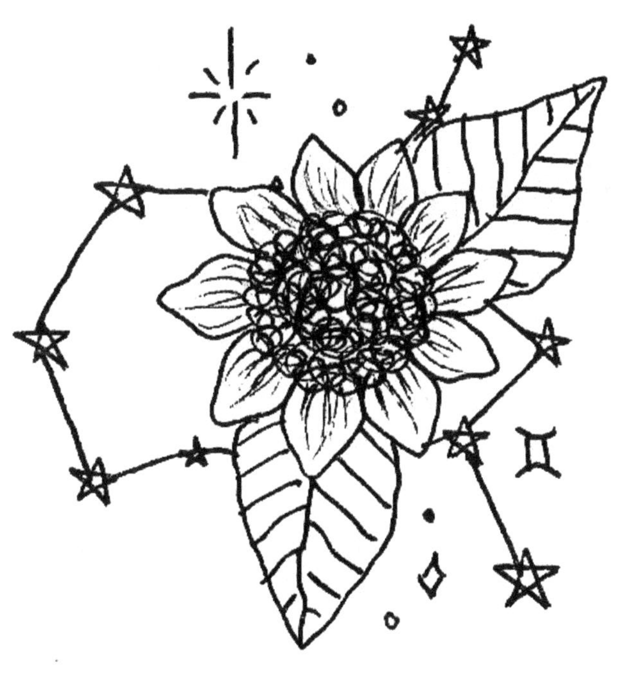

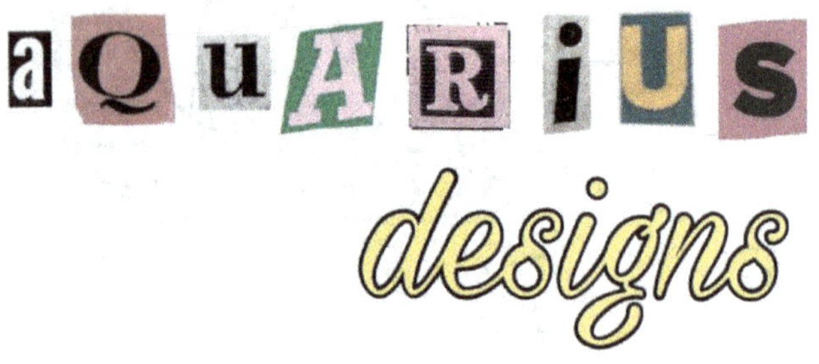
aQuARiUS
designs

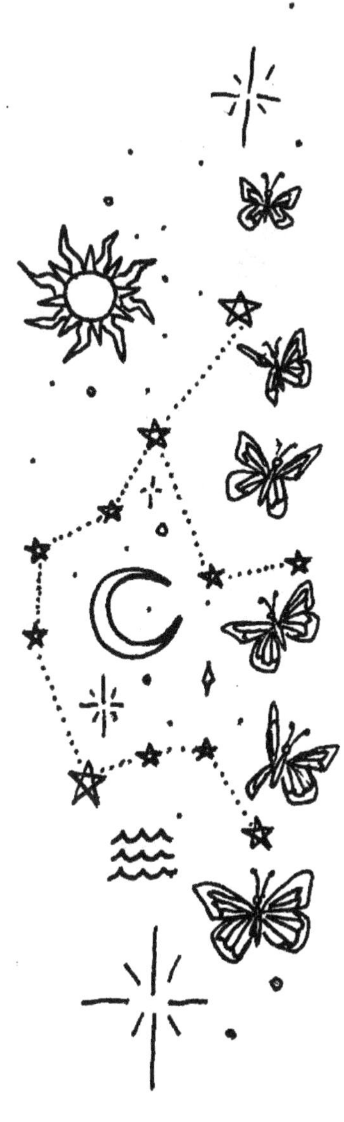

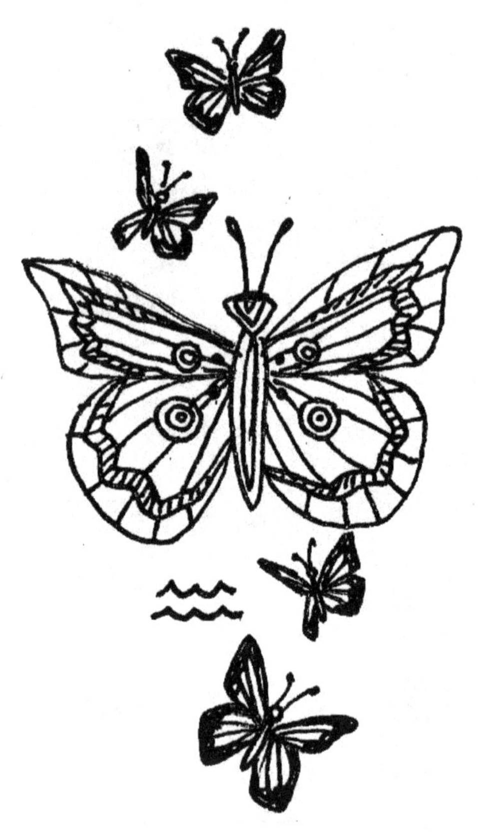

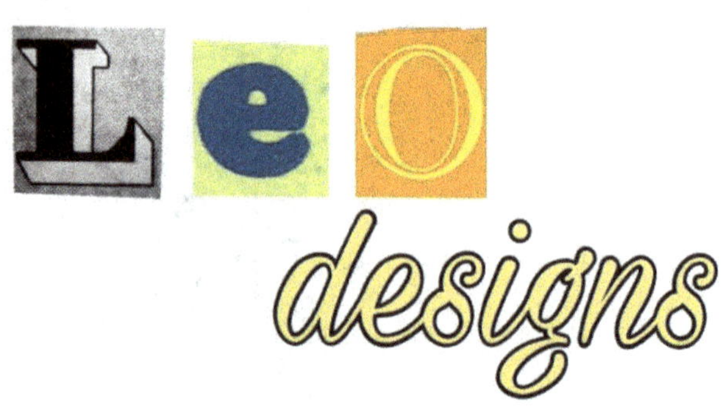
LeO
designs

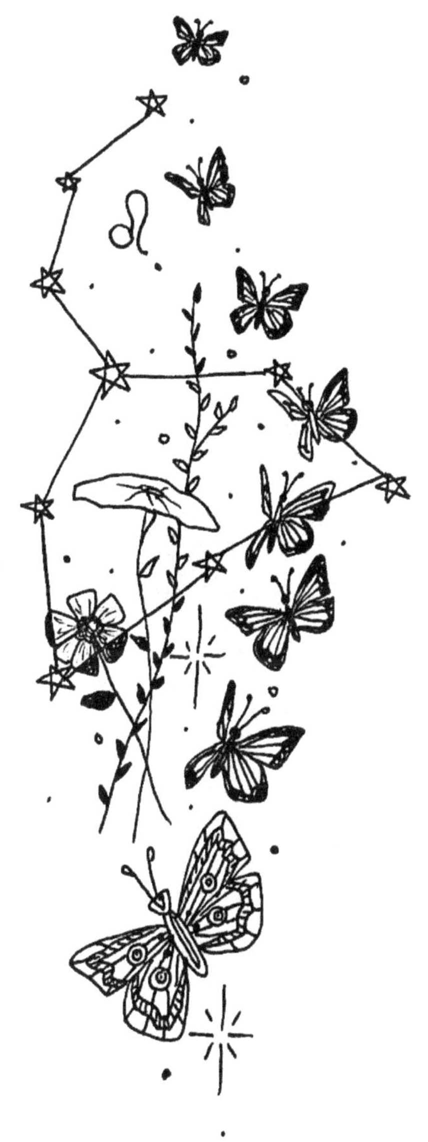

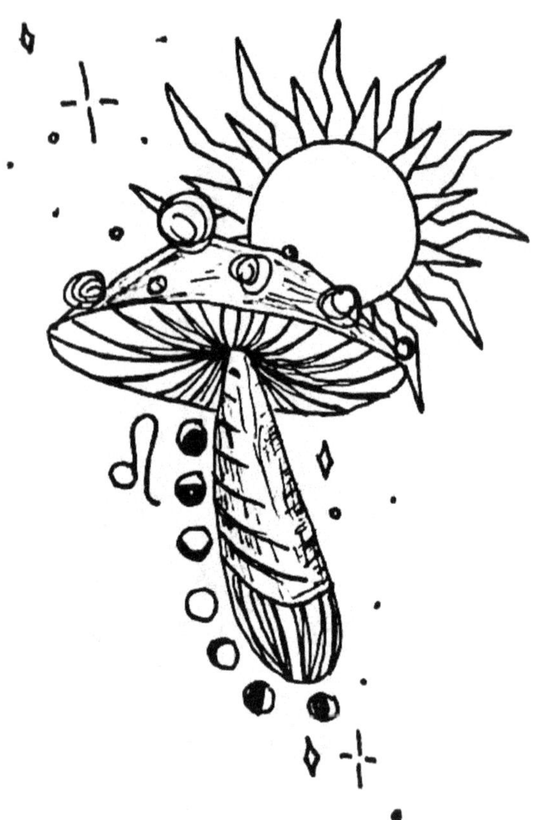

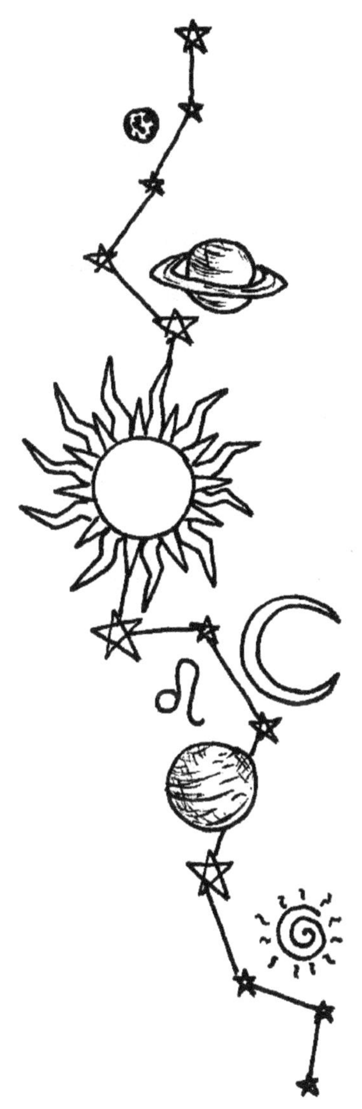

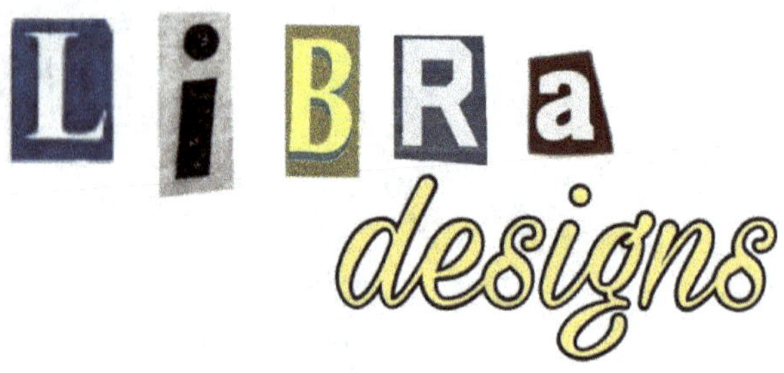
LiBRa
designs

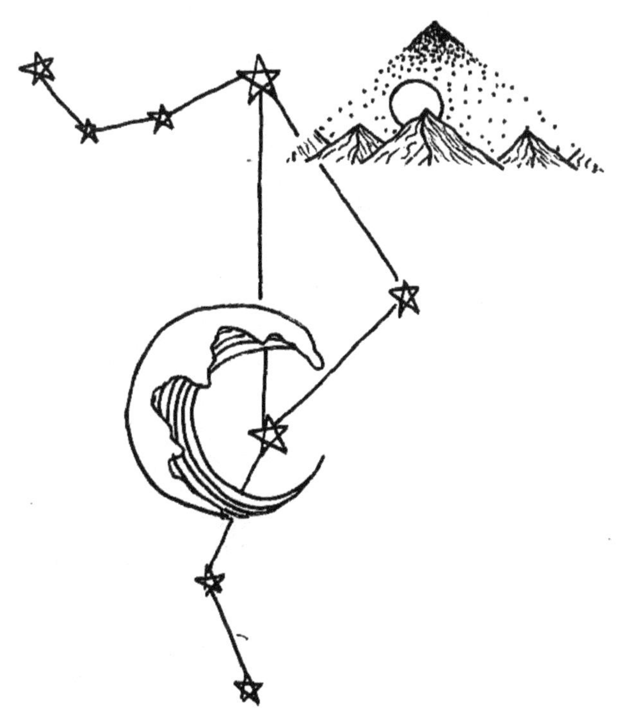

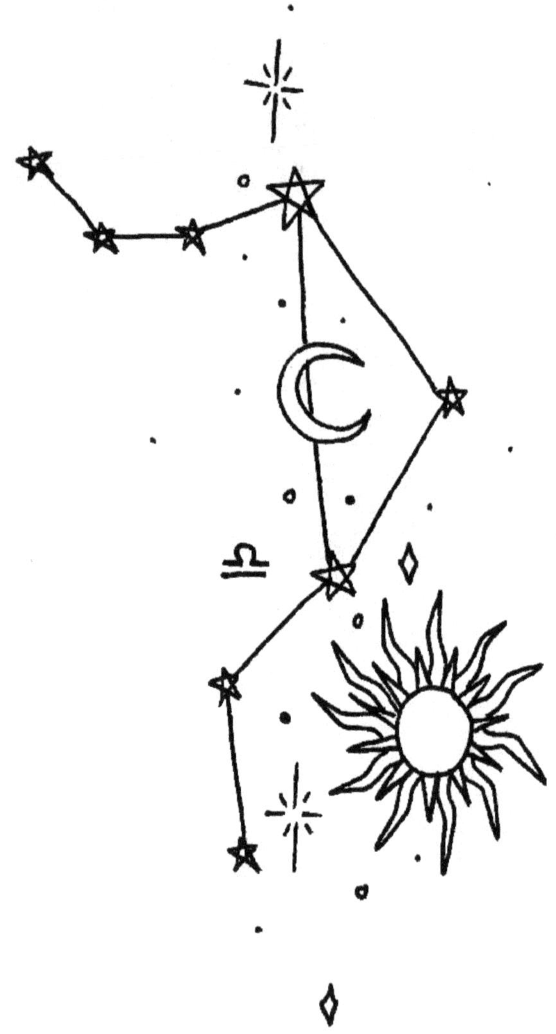

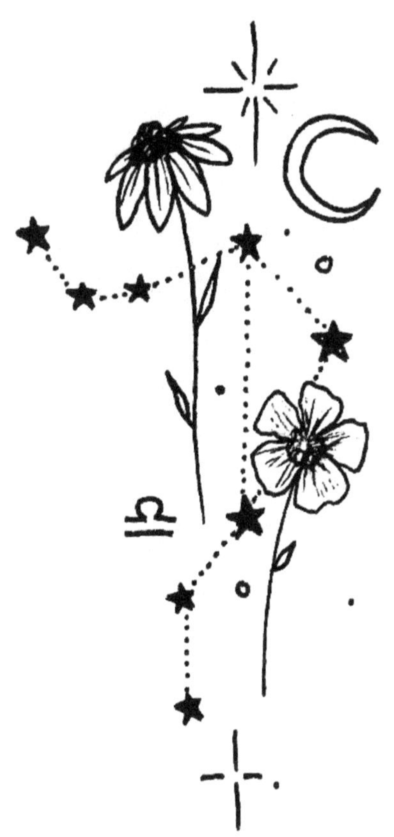

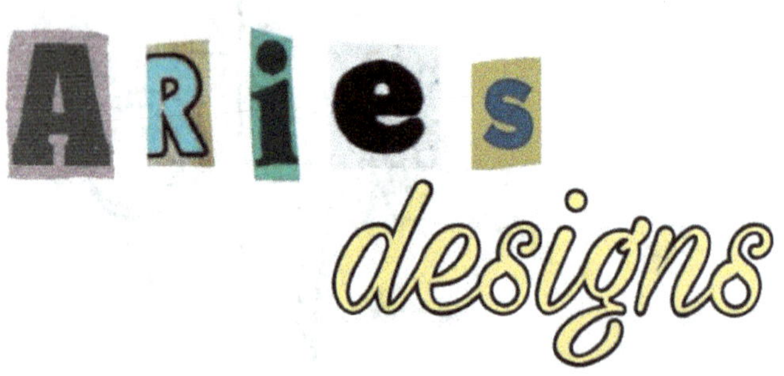
ARies
designs

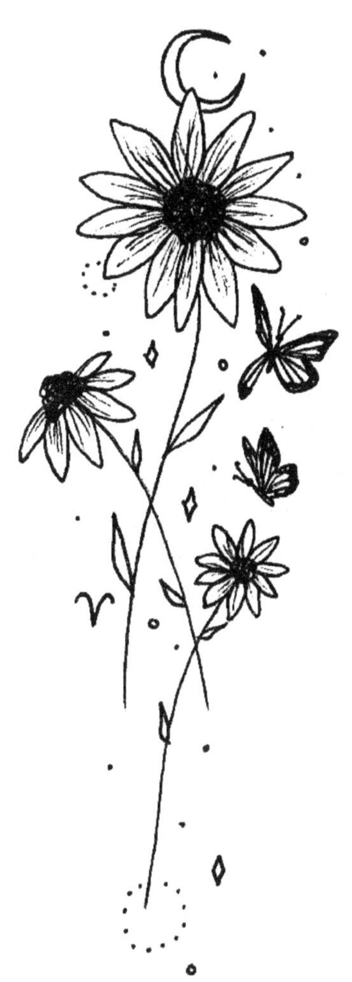

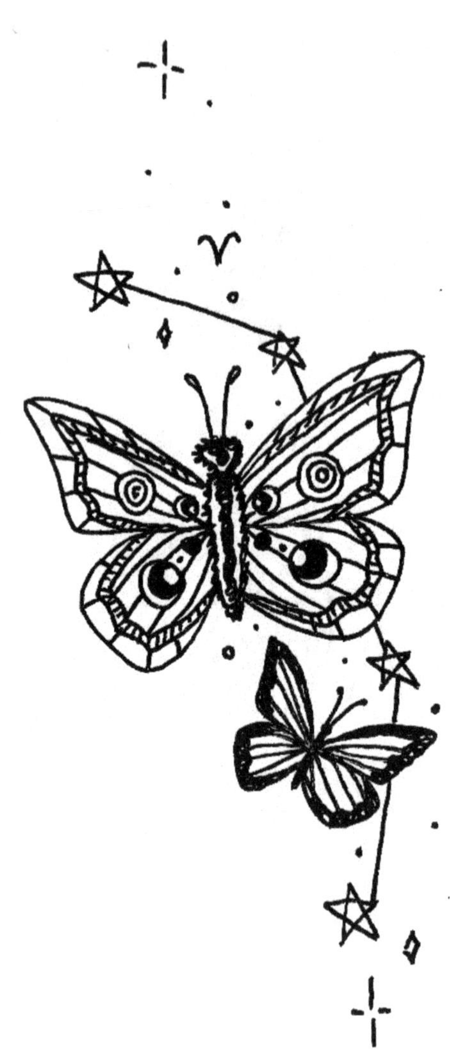

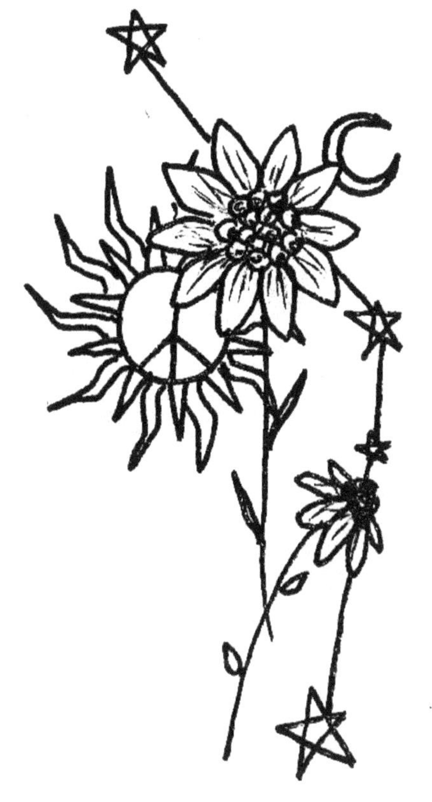

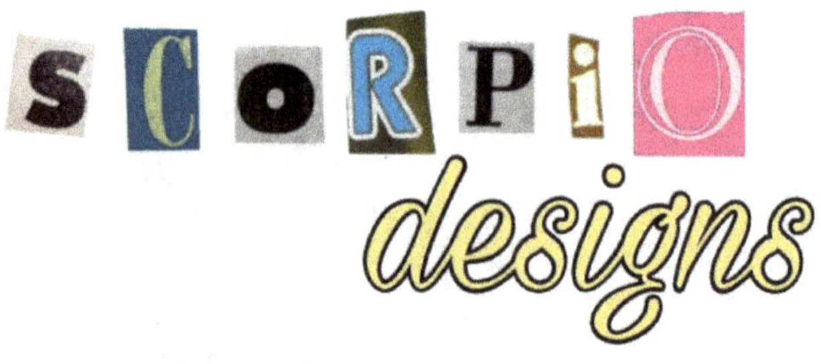
SCORPIO
designs

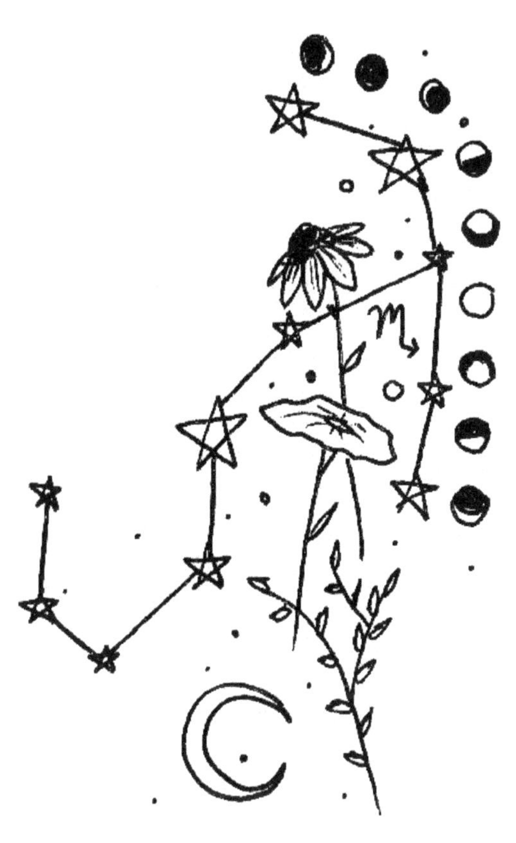

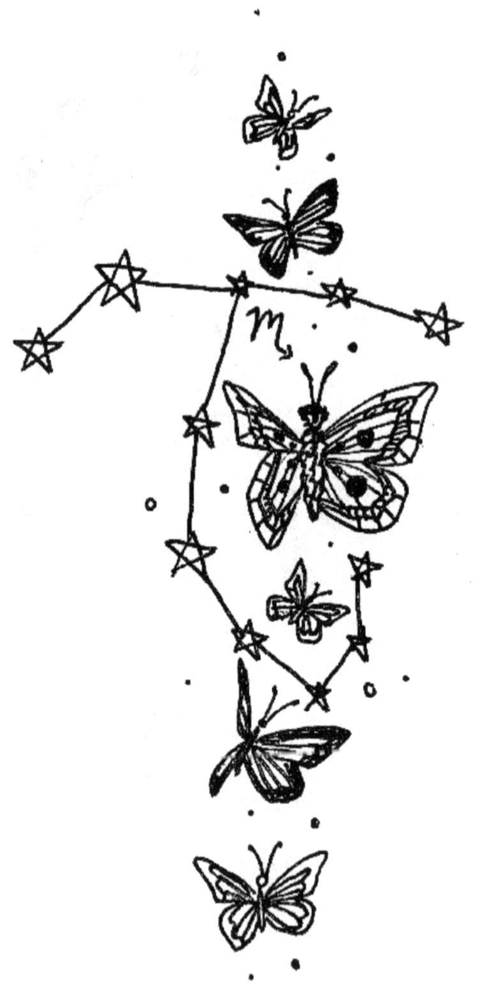

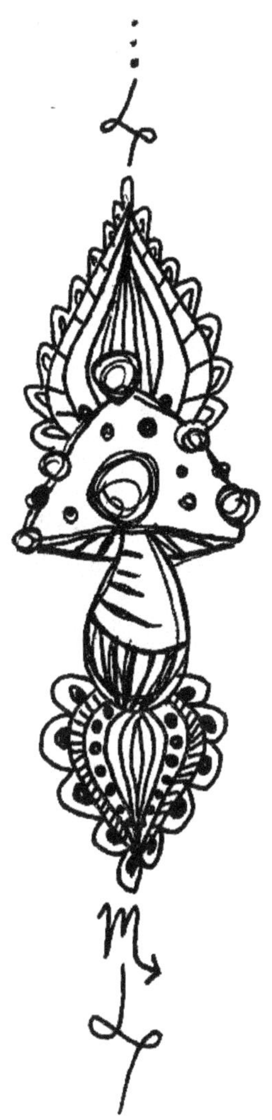

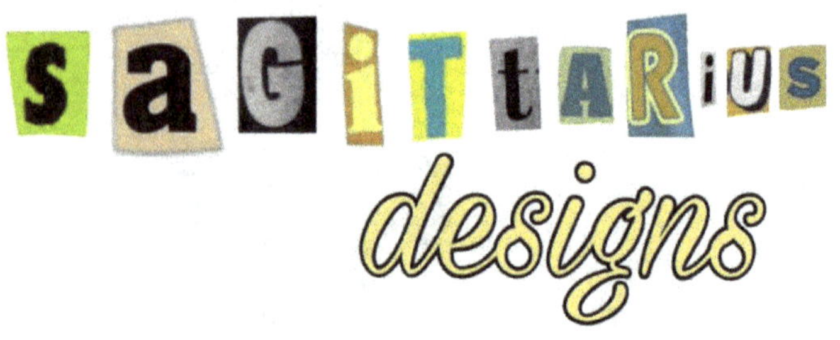
sagittarius
designs

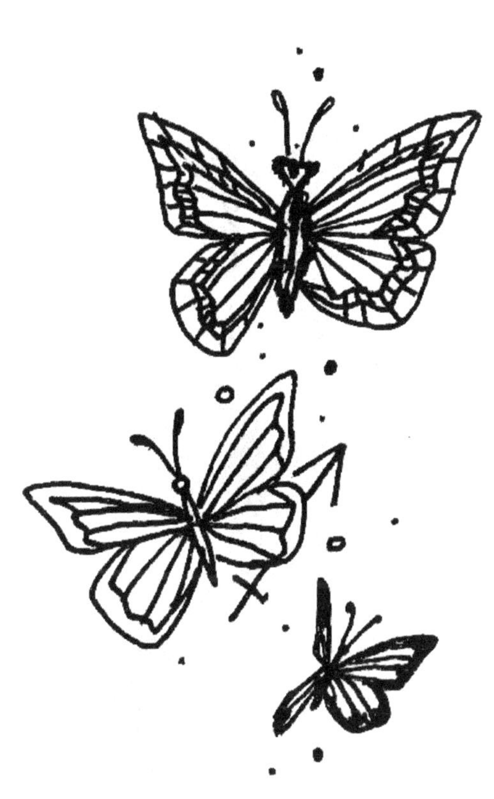

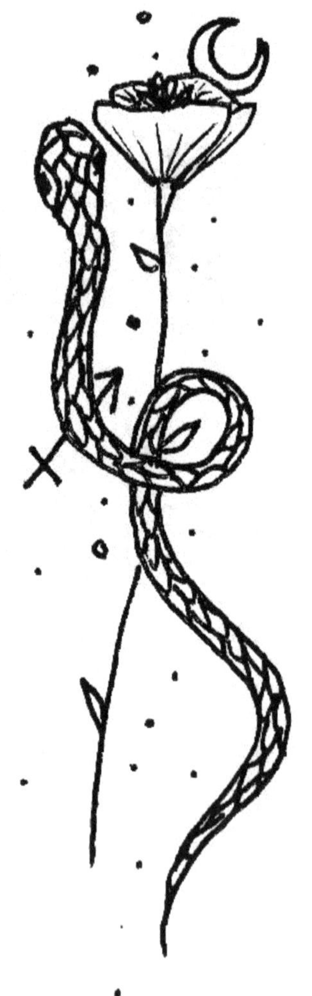

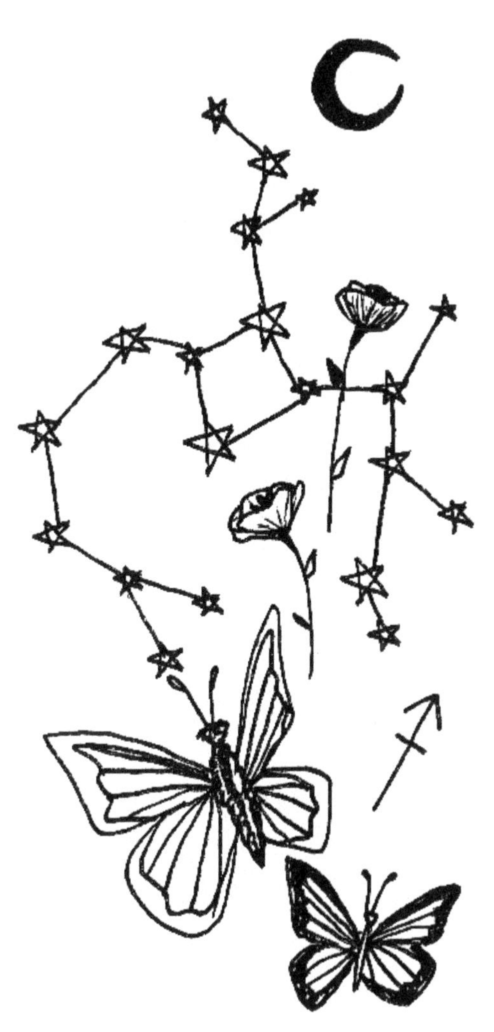

VirGO designs

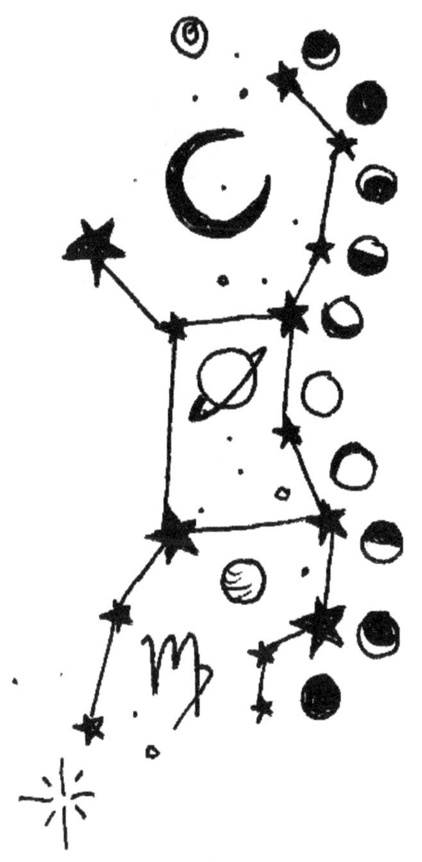

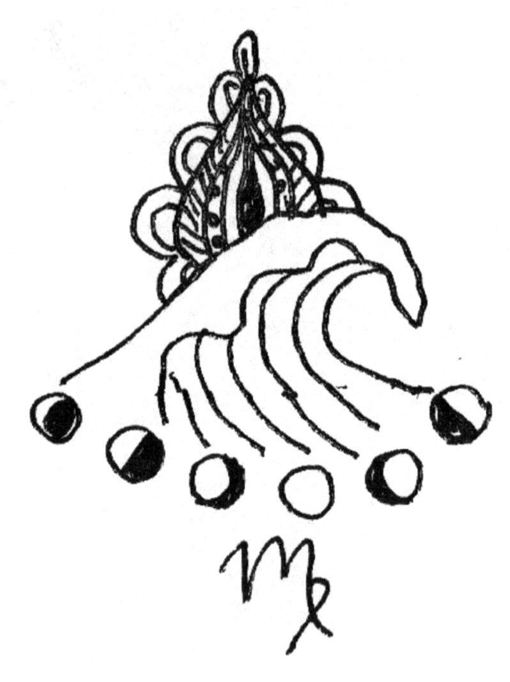

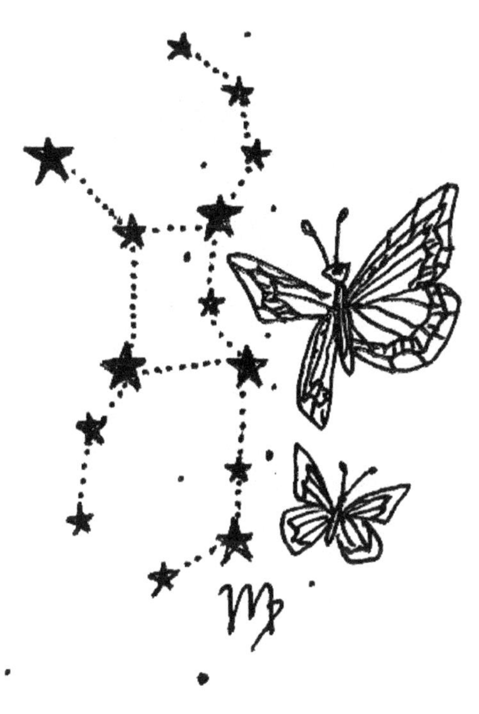

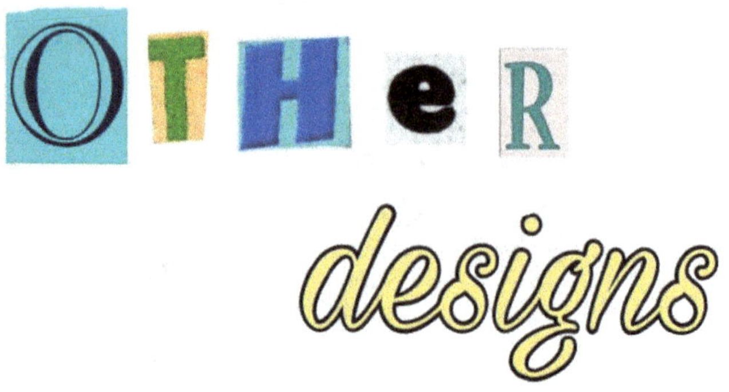
OTHeR
designs

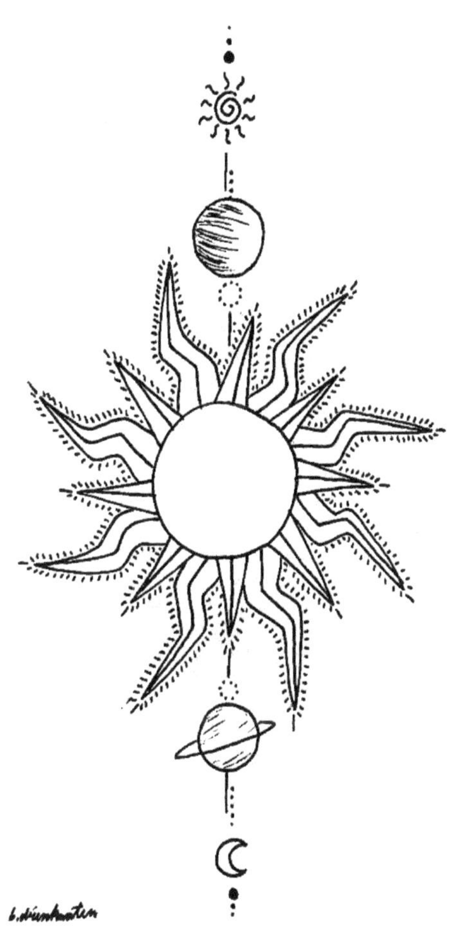

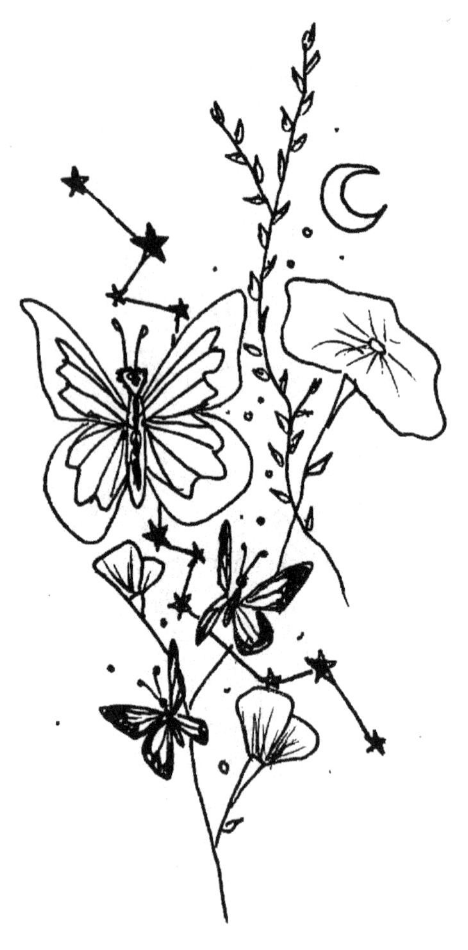

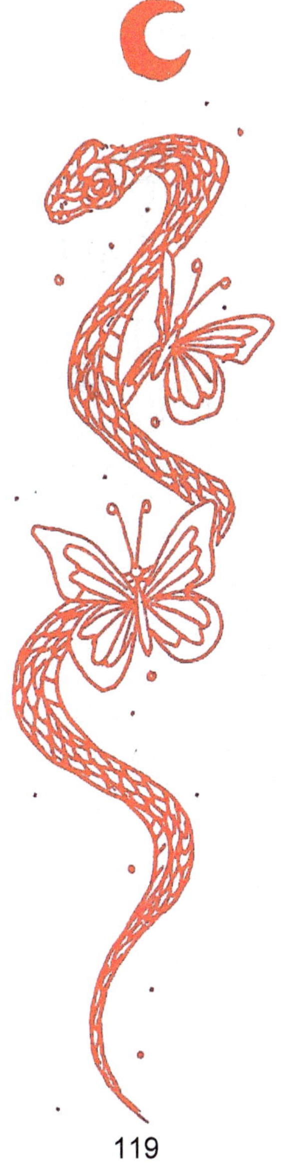

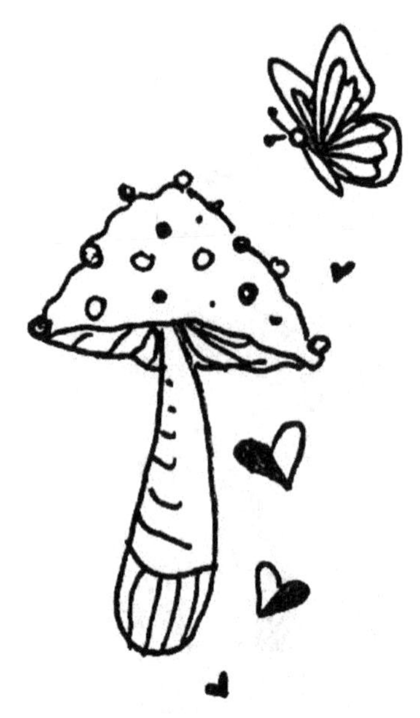

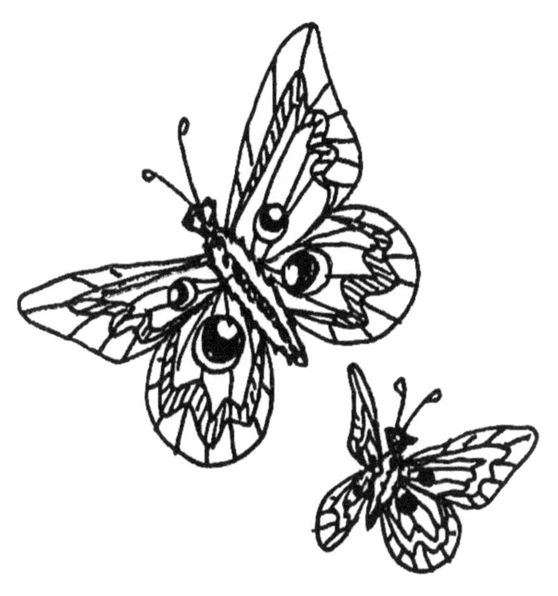

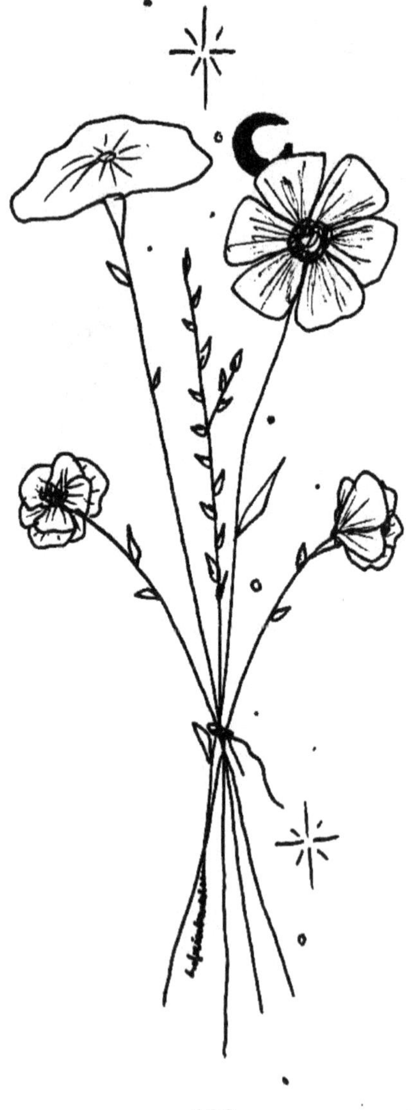

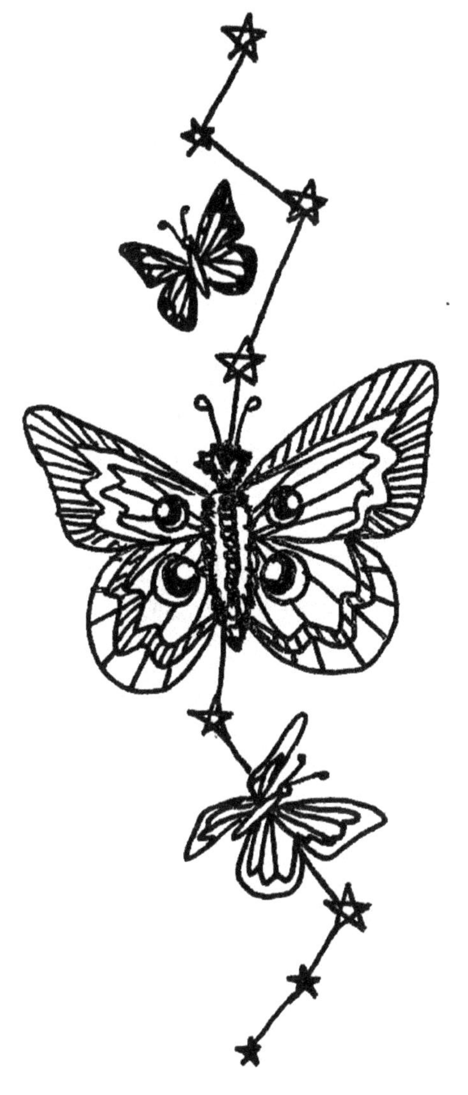

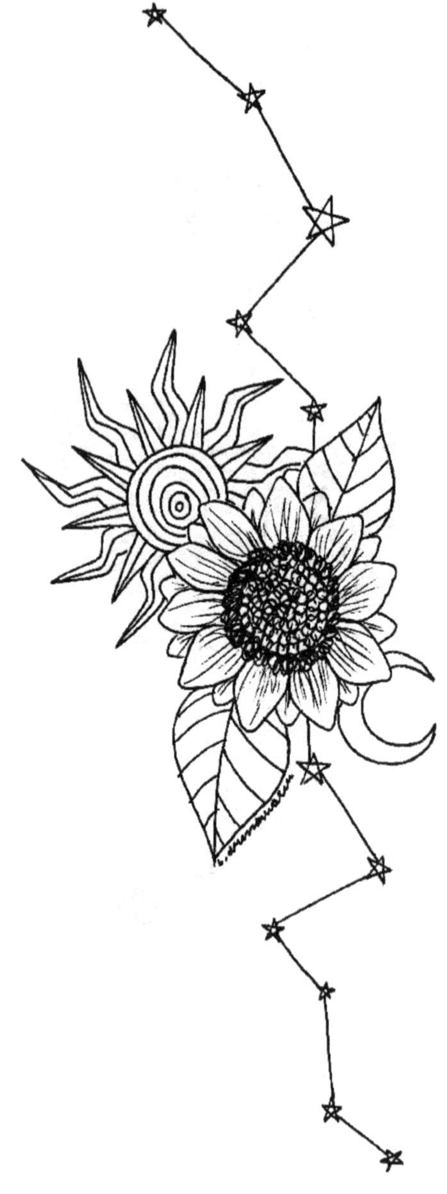

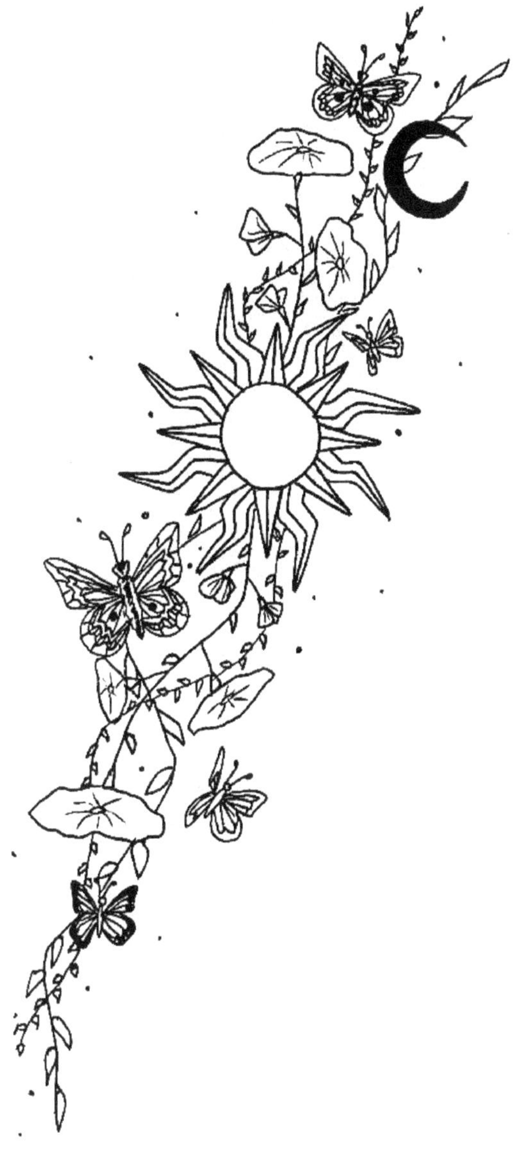

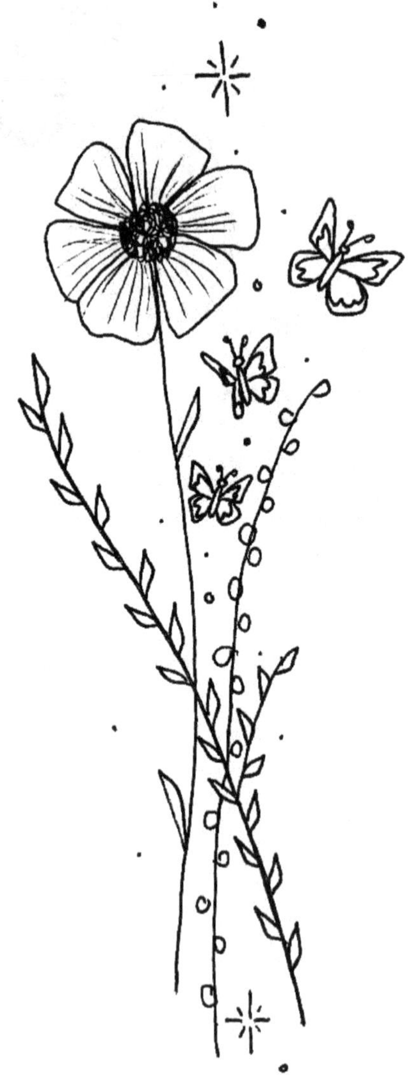

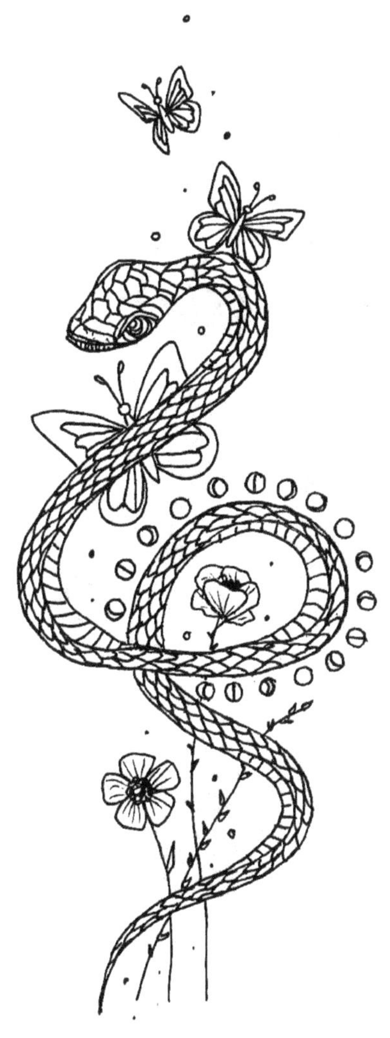

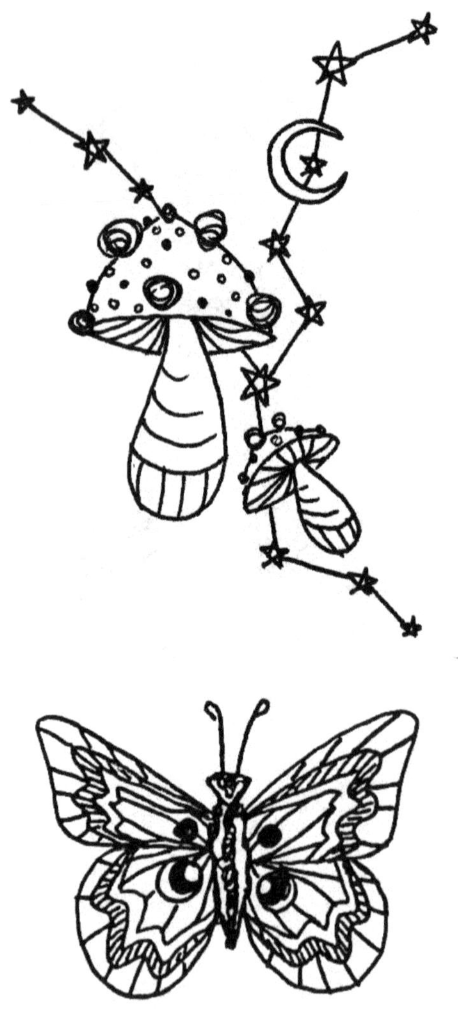

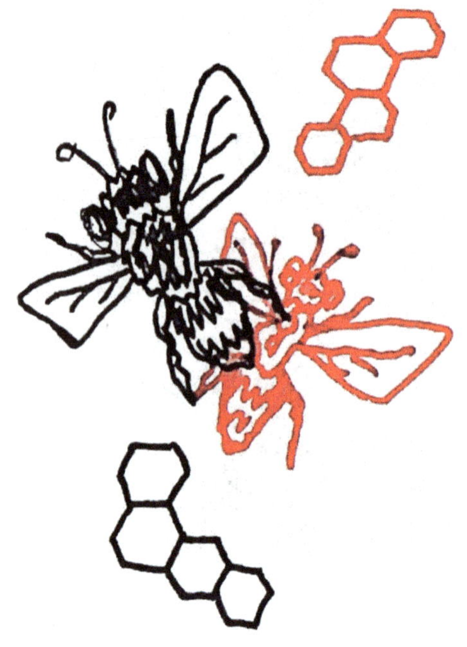

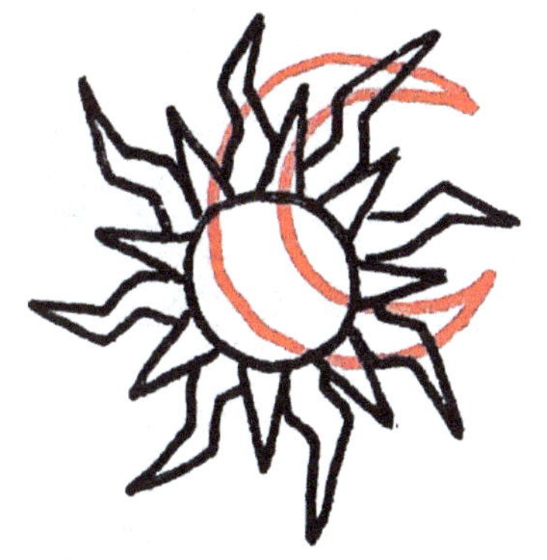

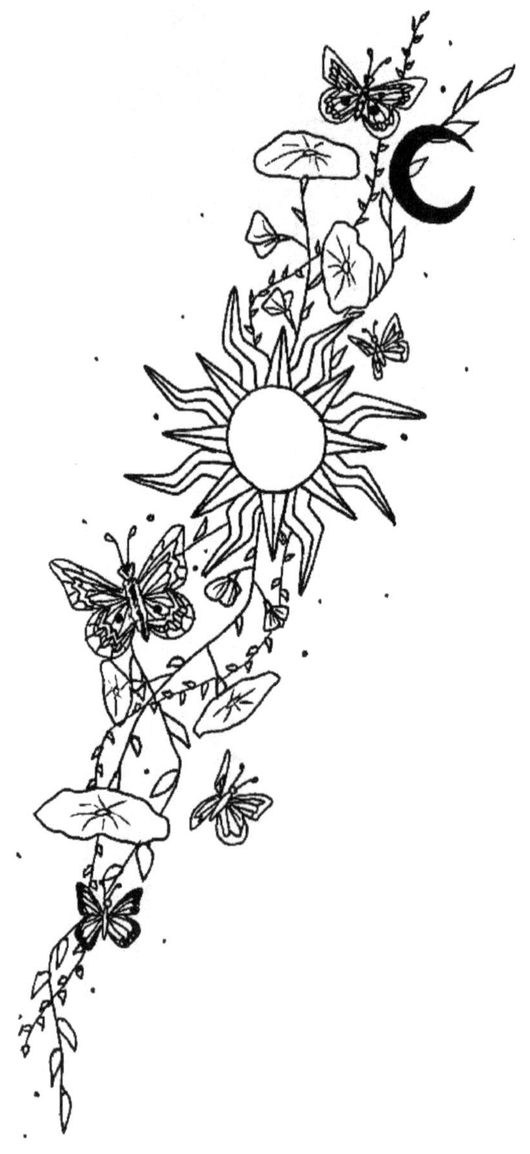

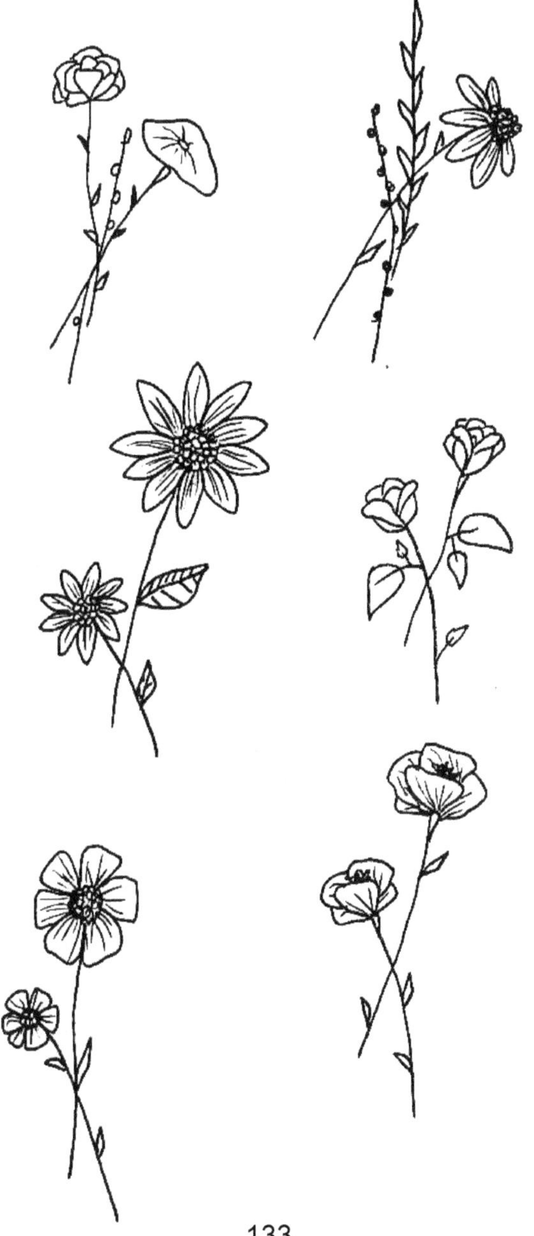

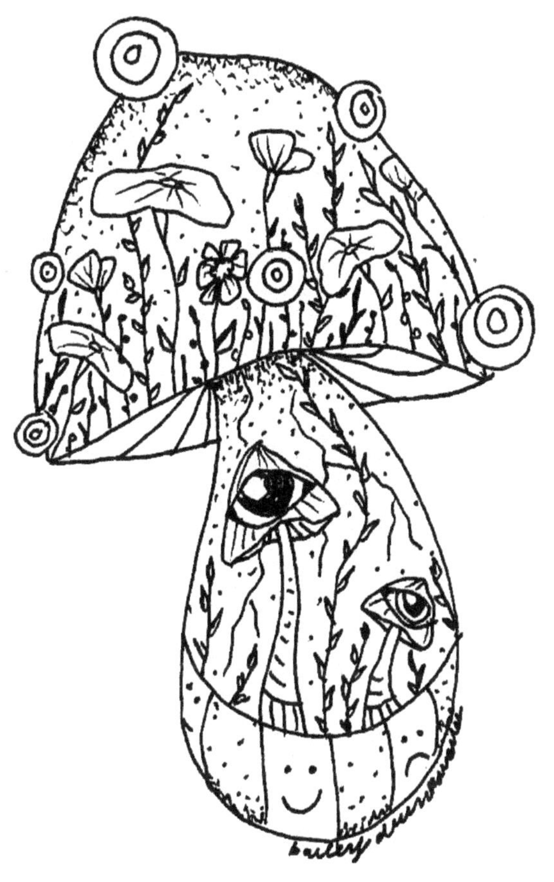

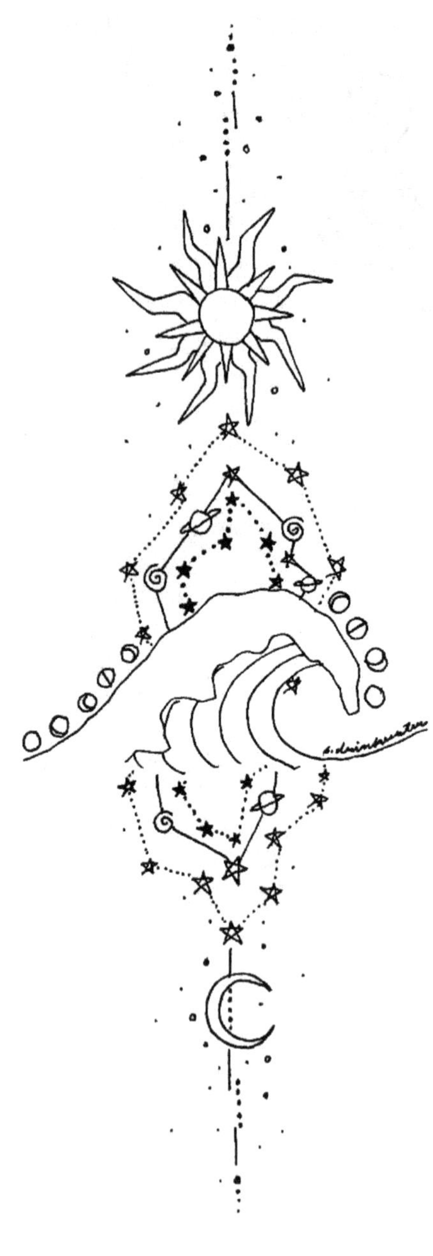

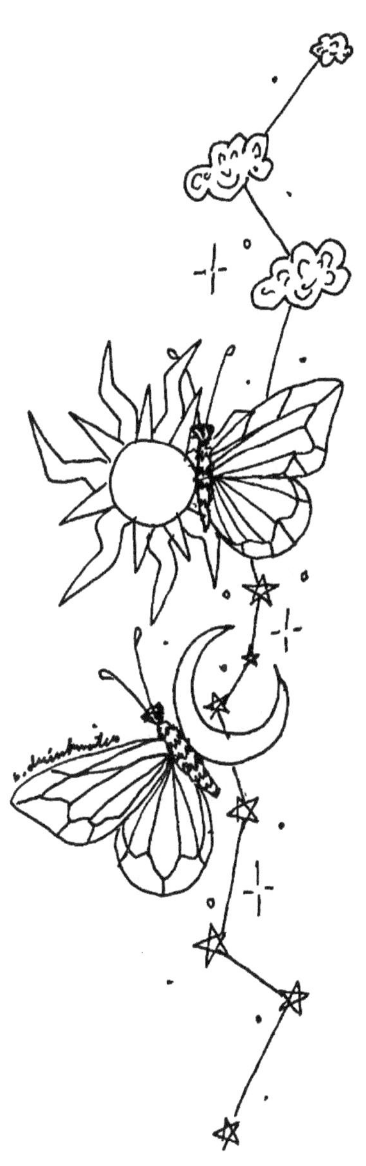

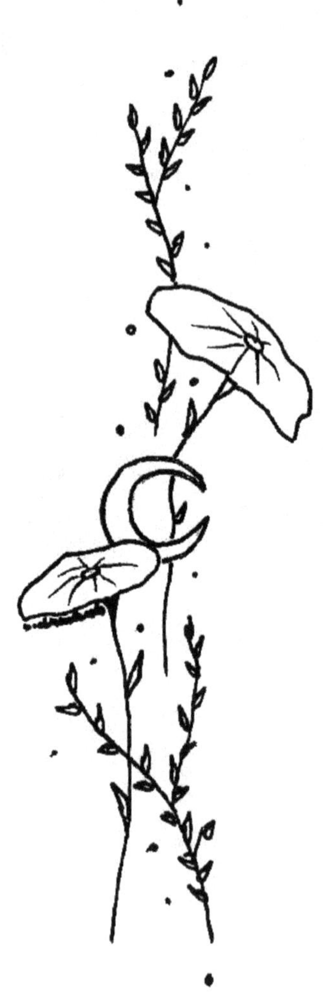

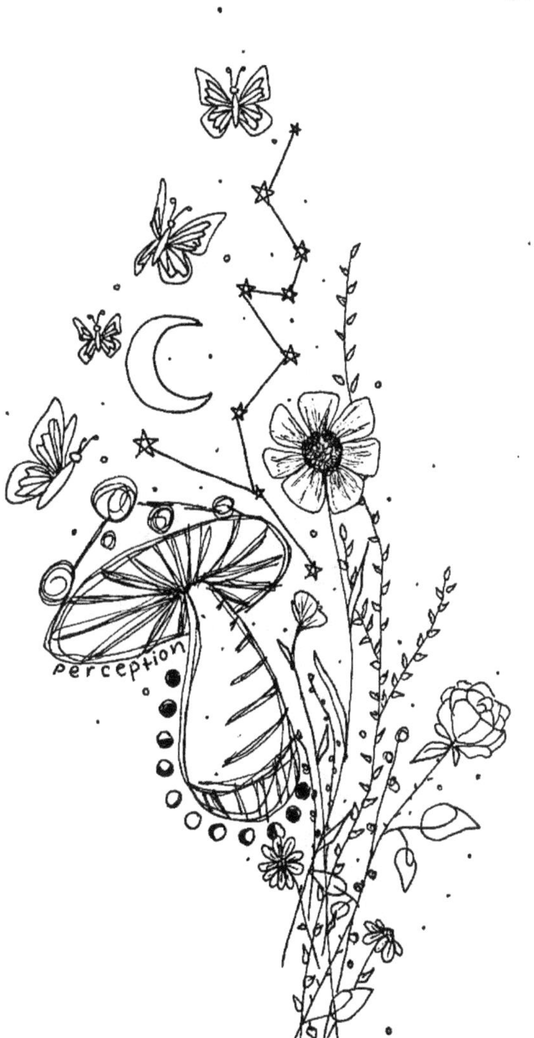

perception

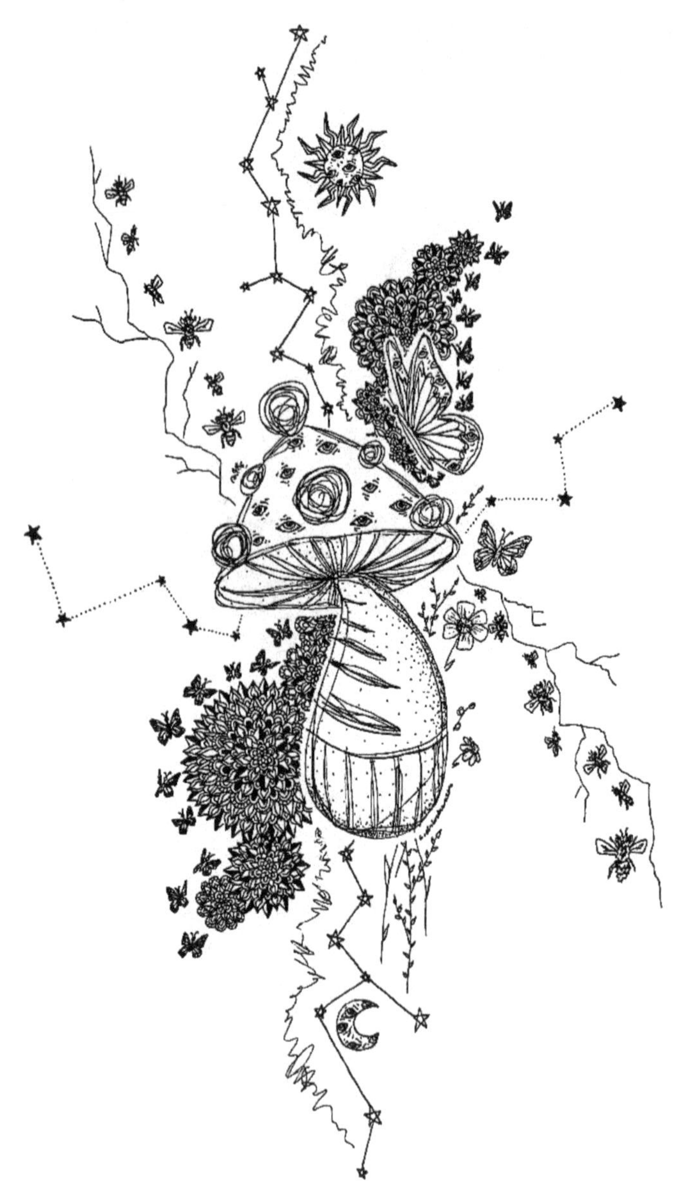

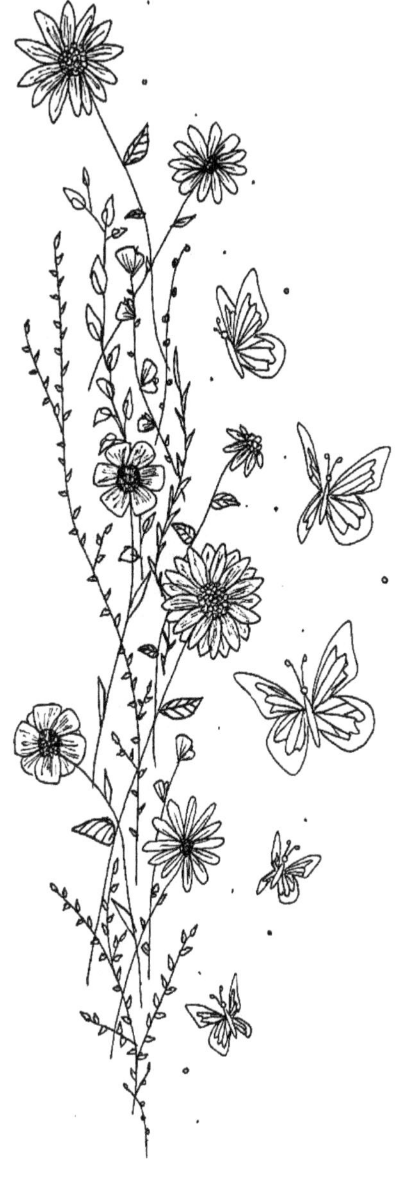

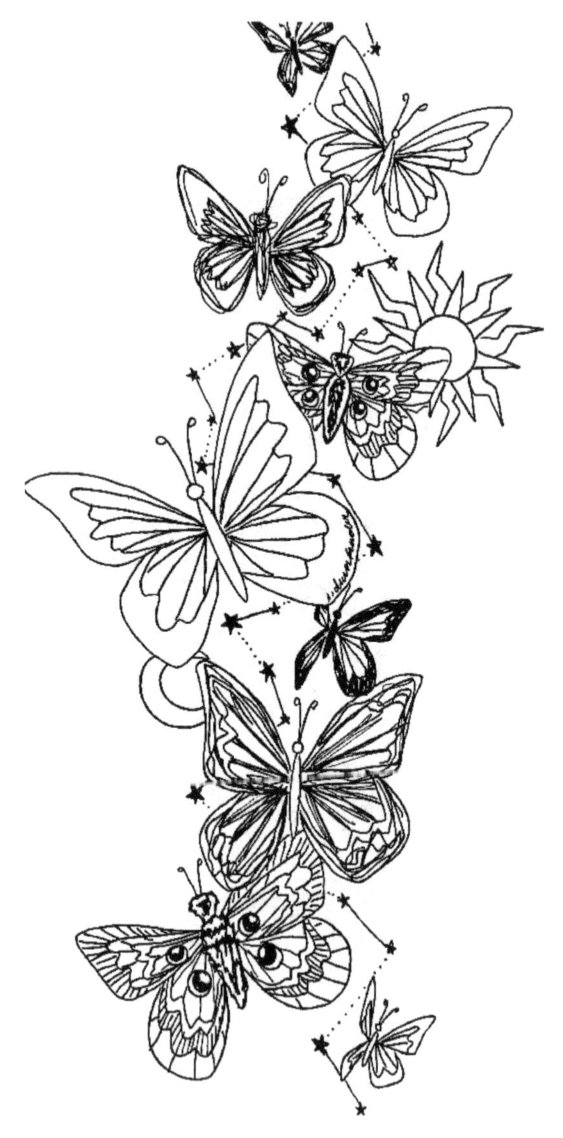

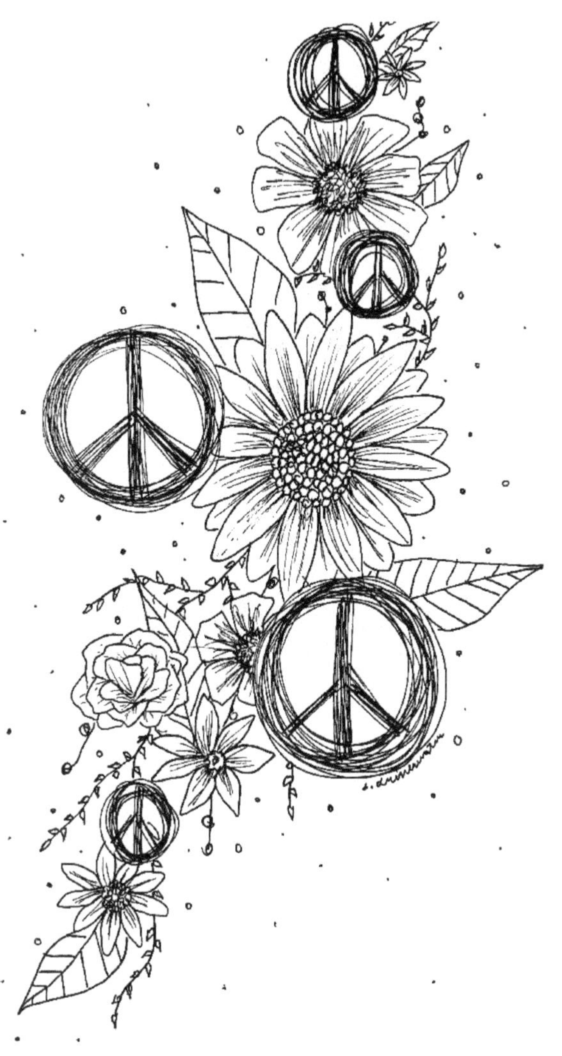

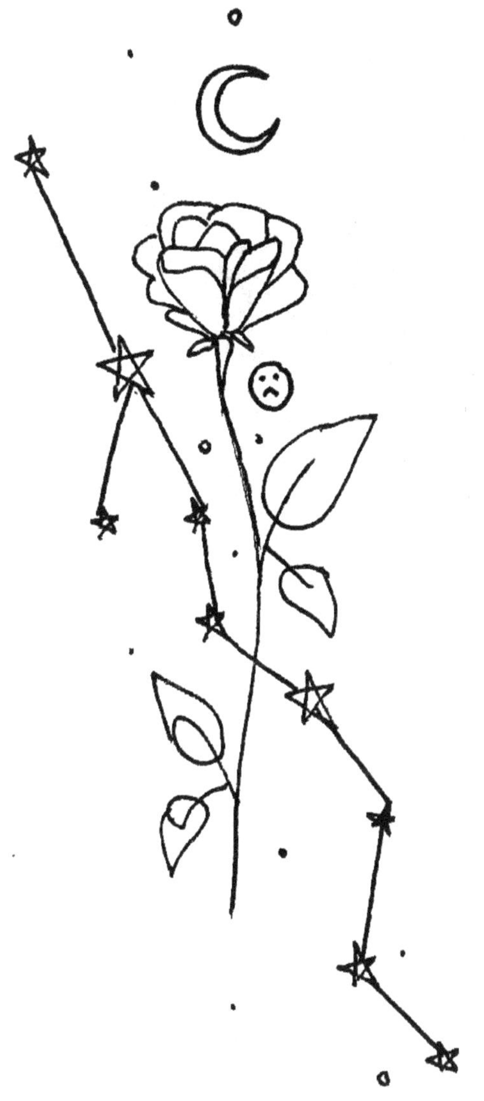

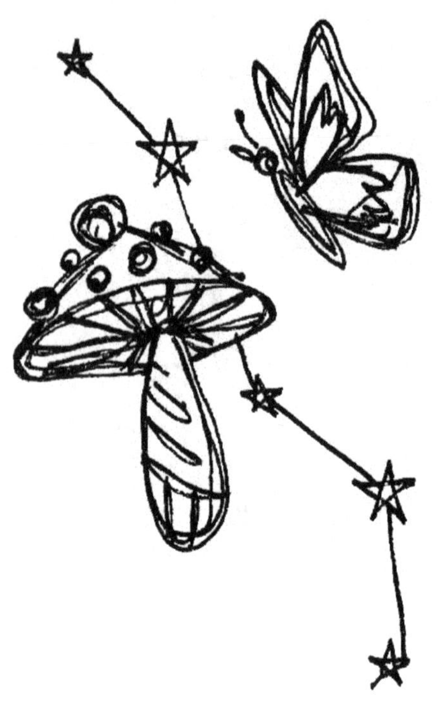

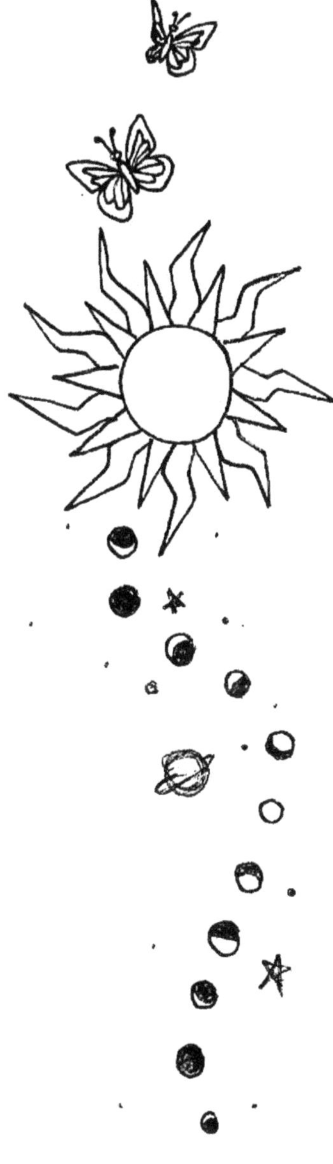

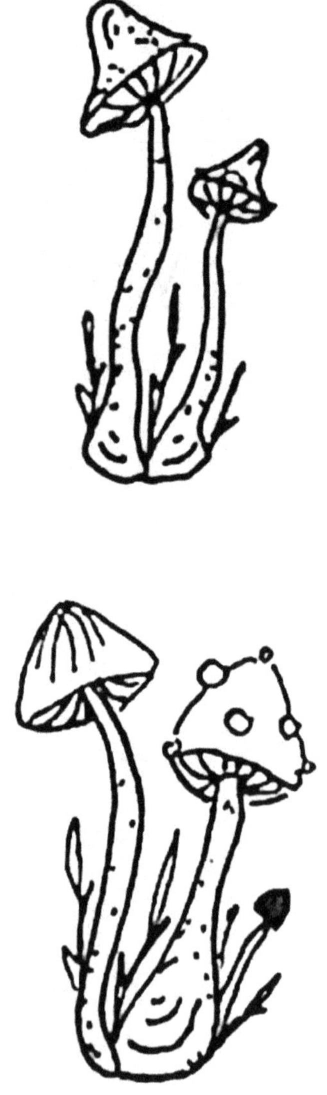

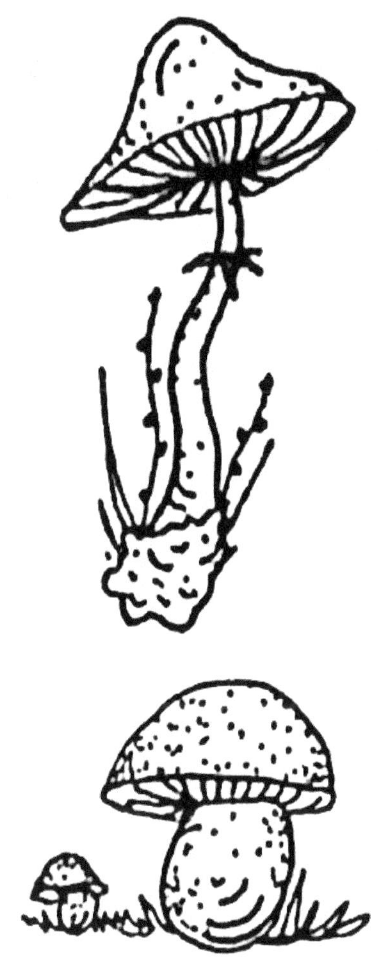

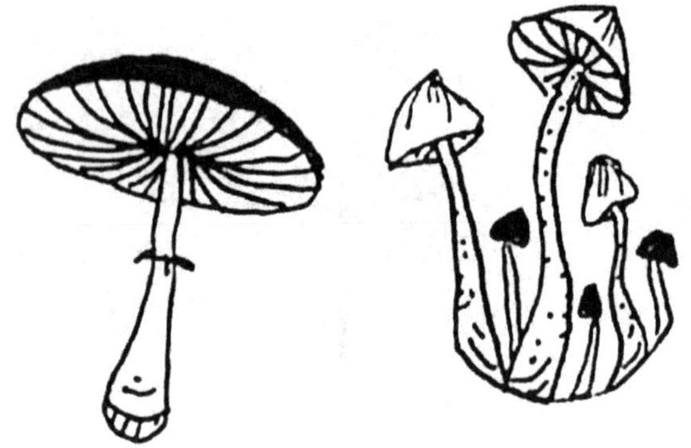

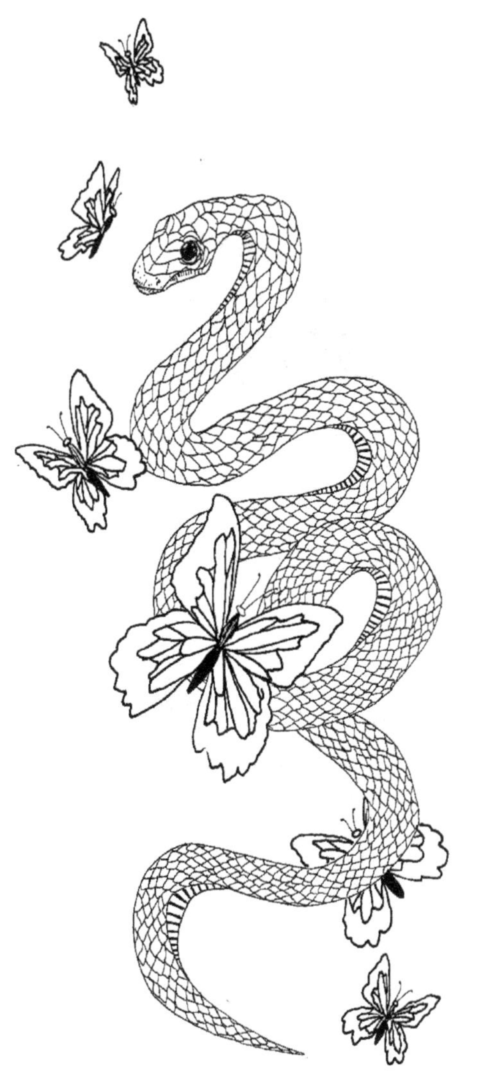

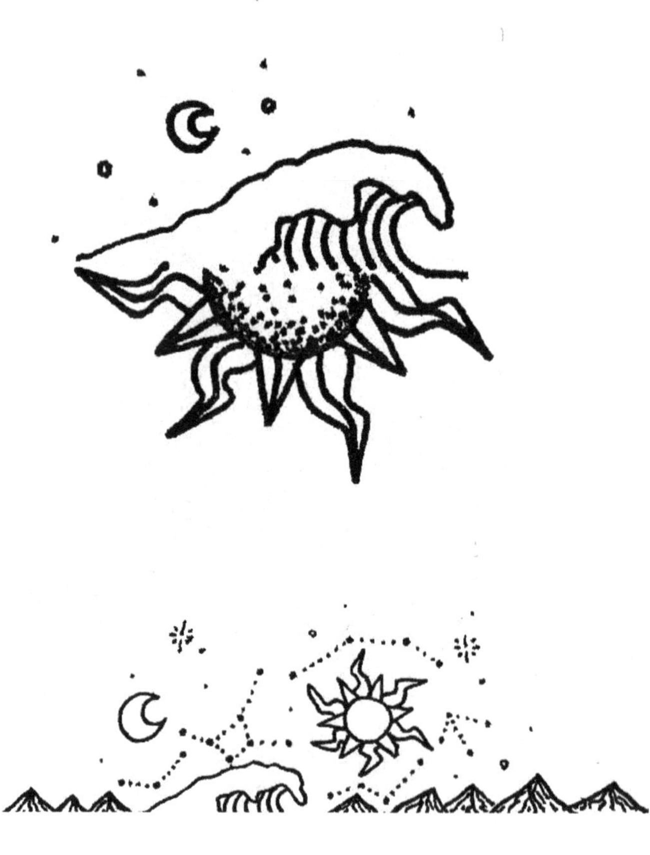

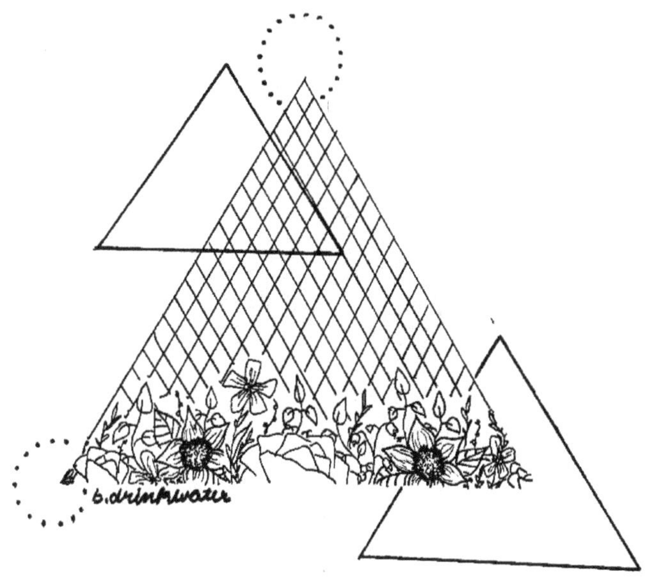
b.drinkwater

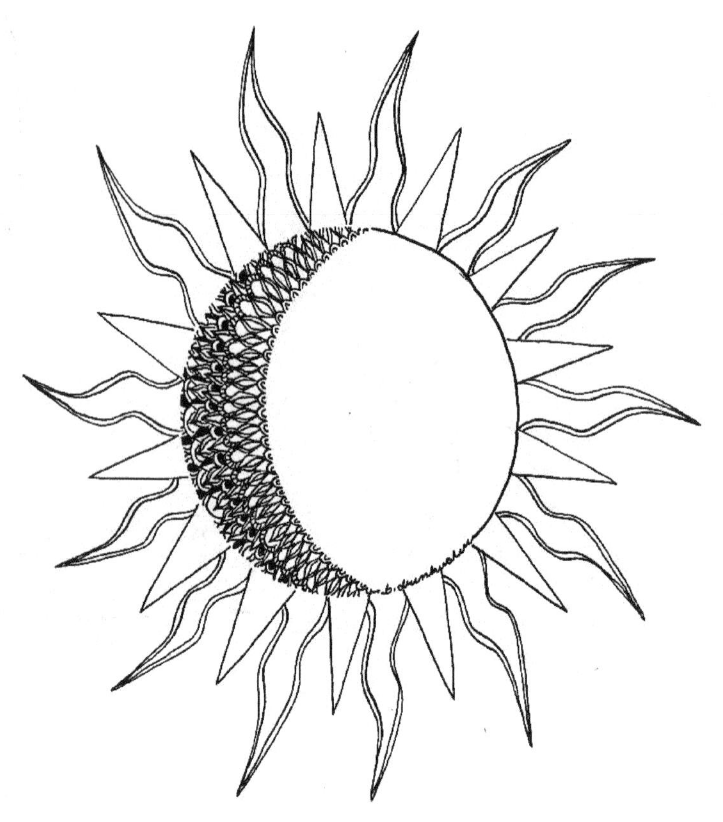

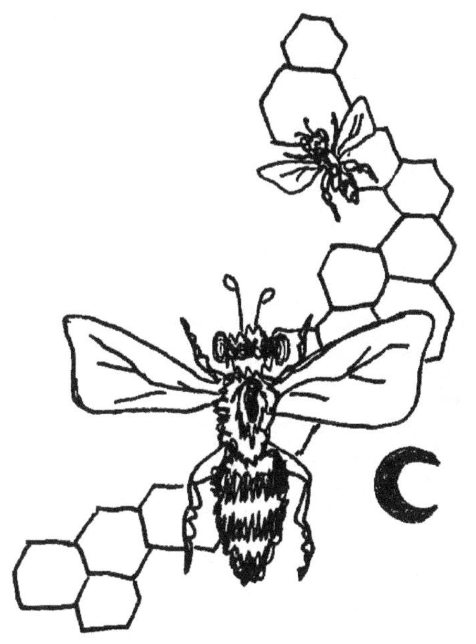

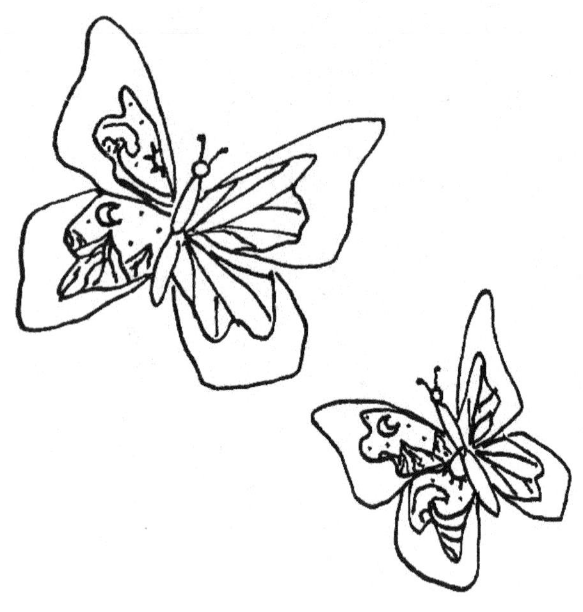

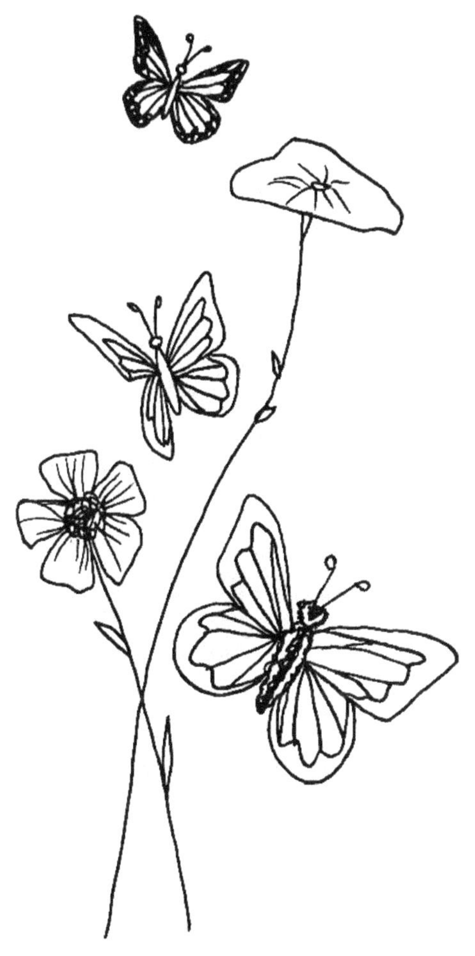

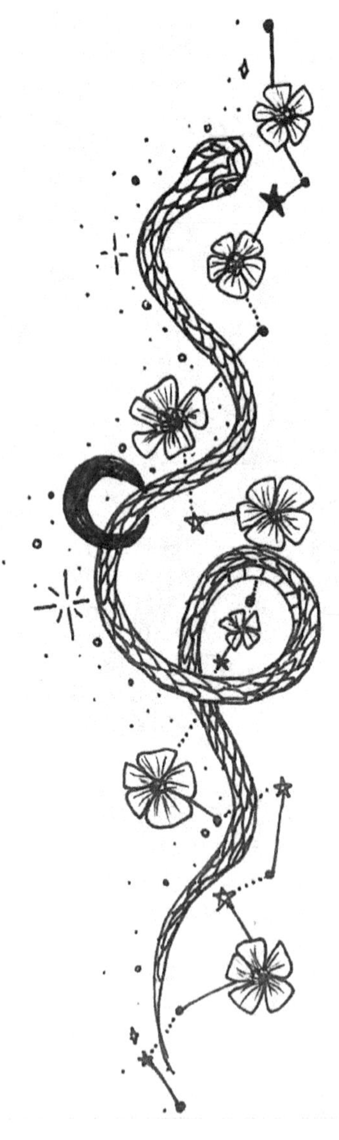

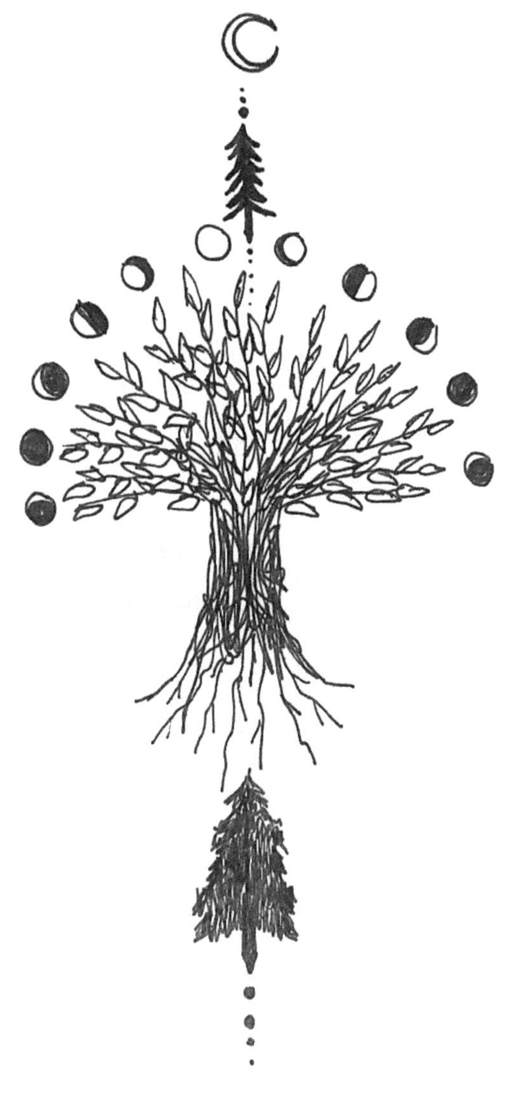

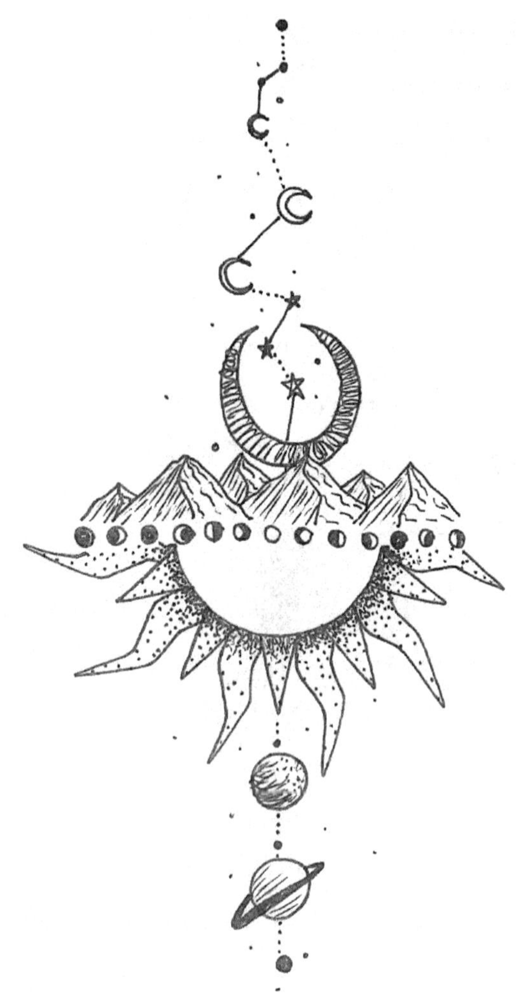

CPSIA information can be obtained
at www.ICGtesting.com
Printed in the USA
LVHW020514280121
677611LV00008B/643

9 781716 334092